Food Routes

Food Routes

Growing Bananas in Iceland and Other Tales from the Logistics of Eating

Robyn S. Metcalfe

The MIT Press
Cambridge, Massachusetts
London, England

This book was set in Stone Serif and Stone Sans by Jen Jackowitz. Printed and bound in the United States of America.

Library of Congress Cataloging-in-Publication Data
Names: Metcalfe, Robyn Shotwell, 1947- author.
Title: Food routes: growing bananas in Iceland and other tales from the
   logistics of eating / Robyn Metcalfe.
Description: Cambridge, MA : The MIT Press, [2019] | Includes bibliographical
   references and index.
Identifiers: LCCN 2018030683 | ISBN 9780262039659 (hardcover : alk. paper)
Subjects: LCSH: Food supply. | Food industry and trade. |
   Food--Transportation. | Agricultural industries.
Classification: LCC HD9000.5 .M4275 2019 | DDC 338.1/9--dc23 LC record avail-
able at https://lccn.loc.gov/2018030683

10 9 8 7 6 5 4 3 2 1

To my parents, Barbara and Bob Shotwell

Contents

Acknowledgments

Ten years ago, Sean Matlis, a runner-friend of mine in Boston, agreed early one Saturday morning to join me for a visit to Boston's Seaport warehouse district. We were on a quest to find loading docks, trucks, containers, and anything else that revealed how Boston got its food supply. We took our cameras, and I grabbed a notebook in case we saw something interesting. Long obsessed with how cities were fed, I was delighted that I had found someone who would humor me through this quest with the same amount of enthusiasm. Sean got me moving. Writers would never produce books if someone didn't get come along with a friendly prod to get words on paper.

As I entered the research stage of writing this book, I was blessed to have many accomplices. As I traipsed around the world in search of stories about how different cities fed themselves, Lauren Shields introduced me to Parisian markets, Iris Anliatamer got me through the ingredient pathways in Istanbul, Maria Uskova explained how Moscow entrepreneurs were creating a new food system, and Elizabeth Andoh and Makiko Segawa showed me everything that goes into producing a simple rice ball in Japan. Professors McConville, Ferleger, and Wiley at Boston University indulged my insistence that being a food historian was a worthwhile endeavor. Their scholarship and mentorship while I pursued my PhD led me to wonder about feeding cities throughout history. And I am very grateful to Marion Swaybill for sharing her insights and ability to craft a good story.

Many of the workers who feed cities every day, from warehouse managers to sausage processors to truck drivers, invited me to see the inner workings of their operations, These people typically love what they do and find satisfaction in moving food forward through a supply chain.

The University of Texas at Austin provided patient support for this book project and access to its many experts on supply chains, transportation, and logistics. I was able to receive valuable advice all along the way. Lamar Johnson, one of UT's supply chain experts, provided feedback on the manuscript from his perspective of the consumer packaged goods industry. Mary Ann Anderson, also a UT supply chain expert, provided access to student researchers Jack Loveridge and Daniel Peacock, who gathered material about how the global food supply chain operates.

Many thanks to my friends who cheered me on, including Steve Coit who came up with the idea for calling this project "Food Routes," and Susan Trausch, an eloquent and humorous writer who assured me that I wasn't too far off the mark and encouraged me as she read through the manuscript. The team at Food+City, a project based in Austin that supports food supply chain innovation, indulged my absence at meetings and missed deadlines as the deadline for this book approached. For their support, I am indeed grateful.

Other Austin supporters include Brittany Solano and Rachel Laudan, Addie Broyles, and Paige Blake, all patient listeners to the book's story as it unfolded. In Maine, Julia Jahr-Olivas listened to the trials of book writing as we ran miles of mountain trails.

My editor at the MIT Press, Beth Clevenger, was the true believer in this project from the very beginning. From the start, she saw something in this story and doggedly pushed me to a much more interesting approach. And finally, my Austin editor, Sarah Weber, who provided a steady hand and calm tone as she produced one set of milestones after another, figuring how to navigate that sliver of a difference between insistence and forgiveness. Somehow she got it done.

And to my family, I am so grateful for their support and encouragement. Never a week went by when they were not all in with their enthusiasm. Thank you, Bob, Julia, Max, and my dad, another Bob.

Introduction

In 1994, my family moved from Silicon Valley to Mid-Coast Maine. We left monotonous sunshine for capricious, complicated weather. We had just spent a year in England and returned to California inspired by Britain's rural landscape. So inspired, in fact, that we moved to Maine and bought a farm. But not just any farm. We had seen the farms in England that raised historic, rare livestock breeds, and we decided to follow suit. Ours was a conservation farm with a mission to increase the populations of historic livestock breeds in North America. The move seemed like a random impulse, and it was, sort of. But it was consistent with our desire to trade the indulgent lifestyle in Silicon Valley for an unknown adventure in the liminal landscape that lies between Maine's coast and its languishing agricultural interior.

With our two young children, we set up a working farm that would raise heritage livestock as a conservation project. The idea was to increase agricultural biodiversity by raising farm animals that represented genetics that were rapidly disappearing from farms around the world. More genes meant more resilience and redundancy for our food system. Rare livestock breeds survive in dwindling, fragile populations, but by increasing their numbers, we would strengthen and diversify the safety net in case the few commercial breed populations we all rely on ever collapse. Although many of our livestock breeds were no longer commercially sustainable, we thought they might be of interest to a few chefs who thrived on new, scarce ingredients for their menus. We were optimists.

We ran the farm for ten years, soldiering on during long, blustery New England winters. Grocery store managers and chefs in our town were skeptical. Our closest high-end restaurant bought lamb from New Zealand, but not from our farm three miles away. We did succeed on other fronts. We reestablished Gloucester Old Spots pigs in North America after the breed population had dwindled to only four animals. Now the breeding population is about two hundred in the United States. Still fragile, but at least still on the map. We also established heritage breed programs on many other US farms while introducing them to chefs in the Northeast.

After ten years of operation, the farm's model—based on small populations of animals—was unsustainable, so we paused our efforts to bring attention to dwindling agricultural genetics. We eventually sold the farm, passing on the animals we'd raised to other farmers, who we had encouraged to conserve heritage breeds. Our project was too much too soon.

Today, heritage breeds are on the menu, and small farmers find the interest in local and sustainable brands helpful in terms of positioning their products. We have a greater understanding of our food system and a full-bodied language to describe it. When we operated our farm, no one talked of local or sustainable food. Timing is everything, as Daniel Pink says in his book *When*.

Ten years after closing the farm, I began teaching food history at the University of Texas at Austin. It was time to think critically about our food system, and it was finally time to find out why that restaurant in Maine wouldn't buy our meat. The timing of this project was better, but finding the answer has taken longer than expected. We talk all the time about new ways of growing or eating healthy food, but we still don't know much about how we get food to our tables. The answer to why restaurants don't routinely buy ingredients from local sources lies somewhere between the farmer and the chef. In 2011, I organized a project called Food+City to explore how we feed our cities. This book is a product of our work at Food+City, digging into the "to" of "farm-to-table."

You'll find out about this invisible stretch of our food supply chain in this book, but here's a hint about why our food doesn't always travel in logical ways to from farm to plate: New Zealand produces grass-fed, uniform lamb all year long at a fraction of the cost of our farm's lamb in the United States.

We are witnessing major changes in the way we grow, process, transport, and consume food. Each change that occurs within our global food system sends ripples throughout the supply chain, up and down, back up to the producer and back down to the consumer. These changes will result in getting better food to more people while lessening the waste and environmental impact along the way. Networked, digital tools will both improve our food system and challenge our relationship to food in new ways, not always with positive results. We need to recognize this tension and anticipate our response to the increasing use of technology in our food system.

Who are we? Mostly likely the readers of this book are able to afford to think about where their food comes from, the environmental impact of our global food supply chain, and the problems related to food waste. The food system at the heart of this book is not so privileged. We will investigate the global food supply chain in the broadest sense—feeding 90 percent of the world's population, and not just the readers of *Eater*, the members of Slow Food, and those of us who Instagram our latest foraged dishes.

The food system at the heart of this book needs reinvention, maybe even a total redo, in order to provide enough healthy food to the entire world population now and in the future. We have an opportunity now to use the technological advances available to make impactful changes in the way we grow and distribute our food.

I'm a technology optimist, but I am cautious about how we use technology when it comes to our food system. The optimism comes from our experience producing our annual Food+City Challenge Prize, a competition for entrepreneurs who are starting businesses in the area of food logistics. Applications for the competition increase every year. That's reason enough for optimism.

But as we move toward blockchains, robots, and engineered food, we should keep a wary eye on all the complications they engender—especially when food is involved. We can use technology to improve our financial system or to deliver curated content easily enough. But food goes into our bodies, it can kill us if we let it, and it is all very, very personal. We get all fired up over our grandmother's apple pie or our town's world-famous chili, in spite of the carbon footprint of the ingredients. Our food tells the world who we are. Will changing our food system change who we are? Or are we changing in ways that will shape the future of our food system?

The purpose of this book is to challenge our current assumptions about our global food system and to explore what the future might look like.

We've grown accustomed to talking about our food system in terms of opposing values: big food, small farmers, global food supply chains, and local food. Almost every narrative about our food settles into one of these tendentious camps. The latest technological advances are loosening up some of the barriers that have impeded progress toward change. We are challenged more than ever to reconsider our attitudes toward science, art, and what it means to be human.

We've been here before. When the industrialization of food occurred in the early twentieth century, reformers and consumers welcomed lower food costs and an increase in both the variety and the quantity of food. It wasn't until later that the public realized the effects of a centralized food system that relied on synthetic chemicals and artificial flavors. We're about to get what we wish for again: new digital tools will allow us to follow our food throughout the supply chain, and engineers will make new proteins that may make juicy steaks a thing of the past. Will it take us too many years to realize that transparency can be misused by bad actors, and the elimination of animal-based protein can result in an imbalance in our domestic food production landscape?

Our global, industrialized food supply chain has gradually changed the way we grow, process, and deliver our food. Industrialization brought us to a moment of reconsideration, and we're there again—in an even bigger way—now that the digital revolution has arrived, causing humans to weigh the benefits and costs of being connected through our smart phones.

While we want healthy food we can trust, we also want personalized food and lots of choices. We want the peaches from the farmer next door, one hundred types of bread, fiddleheads from the forest, and dozens of coffee options. We want small, beautiful, slow food at the same time as we want inexpensive, fast, predictable food. The question of how to develop this all-inclusive supply challenges even the most nimble and precocious food systems planners. We will need computers, networks, and software to satisfy all of our needs and desires.

Could it be that the world already produces enough food and will continue to do so, and the critical problem is one of distribution? Might we make a dramatic reduction in food waste if we could just distribute more of what we already produce? Maybe these digital tools can help stop the bleeding of food within our global supply chain.

The subject of the movement of food is complicated by the challenge of gaining access to resources that are bound by confidentiality, intellectual property, and the connections between food security, transparency, and national security. Not everyone in the food distribution system is keen to have their protocols, sources, and future plans made public, particularly when their space is becoming ever more unstable and subject to disruption. As Amazon, Google, and Uber join traditional players like Sysco, US Foods, and Aramark, competition for new services makes the innovators even more guarded about their plans for the future. Traditional concerns about openness and collaboration make it more difficult to get closer to an understanding of how our food supply chain works now so that we can intelligently apply new digital tools to solve its many problems. This is changing, but trust on both the consumer and producer sides will come only gradually, nudged forward by an impatient market.

You'll find four themes throughout all six chapters in this book: reliability, technology, trust, and adaptability. Our food supply chain depends upon reliable quantity, quality, and schedules. Without technology for production, processing, distribution, and transportation, the supply chain would fail to keep up with our growing, global, urban population. Without trust between the source, the consumer, and everyone in between, more of our food would end up in landfills. And without the ability to adapt to change and disruptions, our food supply chain would fail. Our supply chain operates on these four ingredients.

You may find this book's overview of our global food supply chain incomplete. The focus of these chapters is to give a brief overview of how the food supply chain works while describing the changes occurring today and suggesting how they might impact us going forward. Treat this flyover as a primer to the mechanics and dynamics of the subject, and use it to find your way to more specialized books about supply chains and food logistics.

You will also notice the absence of the expected ethical criticisms of our global food supply chain. We're increasingly aware that the food system can appear unjust, insecure, toxic, and exploitive, and that healthy food is simply inaccessible to much of the world. While these observations are valid, they are not the focus of this book. Instead, we'll explore the unexplored, the invisible people operating to feed our cities around the world, the unknown impact of new technologies on the food system. This will be new territory for many of us.

Intended to introduce you to the people and technology that deliver our food from farms to plates, this book begins with a general description of how the food supply chain evolved and how it works today. You should feel uncomfortable with some of the material in this book. Yielding the image of verdant fields of organic tomatoes for enclosed, high-rise green-houses controlled by robots may rattle many of us who feel grounded in soil-grown food.

Chapter 1 moves up and down the chain and back and forth through time, stopping along the way to reveal a little science and a little art and spontaneous adaptation. We'll provide a summary of the basic elements that allow our food supply chain to feed cities around the world.

At no other time have consumers thought of the quality of their meals in terms of location the way they do now, so chapter 2 sets the global food supply chain in the context of geography and distance. This chapter explores where and who produces our food and how we think about the spaces between them. While we will consider the speed of food delivery, we will also explore the complete absence of food delivery in such areas now defined as "food deserts." We'll also review new foods, who makes them, and where our farms may be in the future.

We've become obsessed with distance—sometimes only perceived distance, but mostly the measureable distance between our plates and the source of our food. The idea of a "Food Mile," cooked up by academic studies and government agencies that attempted to quantify the Mile, has turned out to have different meanings for different landscapes. Any given food product includes a number of micro-ingredients, some processing, and the additional journeys to packing, distribution, and storage facilities. All of these stops add distance.

Chapter 3 takes us to all the activities in the midlands of our food supply chain: processing, packaging, and storage. This chapter bridges the gap between the natural food movement and the realities of processing to ensure our food is safe and nutritious. We should admit that all of our food is processed at some point. Critics of our food system often decry "processed" food, but the challenge of serving safe food in a litigious world has raised the stakes for those who want organic, unprocessed food. Shelf life requires some respect since it allows for more food to remain in the supply chain and less food to go in the waste bin. How will we extend shelf life without synthetic additives? And while we resist hyperprocessing of our food, we seem receptive to protein produced in petri dishes, which is processing *in extremis*. This book will explore these new proteins but will save an in-depth exploration of seafood for a later project.

Packaging joins processing as another means for maintaining freshness and extending shelf life (and sending environmentalists into a frenzy, while we're at it). The material between our food and our mouths is the protective layer guarding us against contamination and spoilage. Even more than a barrier, a package communicates its contents and carries the brand's message from the producer. And those packages are communicating in smarter and smarter ways, with more and more labels containing digital information that conveys who produced our food and where.

Food settles in our landscape, stored around railroad terminals, ports, and industrial parks. Grain elevators, warehouses, and cold storage facilities are the silent partners of food logisticians who manage inventories and transportation networks. Some warehouses, such as caves or seafood pounds, are out of sight. Some play strategic roles, storing food supplies in crisis areas or in case of scarcity or environmental disaster. Others hold excess food supplies so prices won't fall below profitability. Innovations like shipping containers have changed the way food is stored in transit, and technology plays a role in most solutions now, from extreme shelf-life requirements for the military to remote storage in space.

Chapter 4 covers the range of transportation networks that connect our farms to our plates. The routes and their hubs take different forms, from food banks to distribution centers. The location of these hubs is often contingent upon the presence of transportation networks; even the cattle drovers located their stockyards in close proximity to the railroads in the late nineteenth century. This chapter explores the four major networks—rail, water, air, and roads—and the networks of the future. Food stored on blimps or in space stations isn't too far off.

Chapter 5 explains how the desire and need to follow our food throughout the supply chain has driven the new innovations around sensors and the Internet of Things (IoT). It illustrates how barcodes, scanners, RFIDs, and GPS technologies are merging to provide shippers and consumers a pathway back to the producer, sometimes in real time. Food fraud, security, and safety create an even more urgent need to develop cost-effective tracking technology to locate food contaminations and counterfeiters in the shortest time possible. The recent obsession with blockchain as the new "killer app" for the food supply chain may indeed create a new option for tracking and tracing the food in our supply chain. We'll take a look at how it works and how some companies are testing out blockchain technology, arguably the most dynamic and potentially transforming link in our evolving future food supply chain. The arrival of new technologies such as blockchain and the integration of food supply chain data will transform the food supply chain. With more transparency and collaboration, the food supply chain will be smarter, faster, safer, and able to move more food to more people at less cost and with less food waste. Feeding cities will be less miraculous and more predictable, saving resources all along the way. This is the root premise of this book.

By the time you reach chapter 6, you'll be ready to take the ideas discussed in the previous chapters to imagine two versions of your food universe: One is an evolutionary future that uses digital tools alongside our traditional food system to improve transparency, quality, and access. The second future is revolutionary, abandoning our current system for one that is engineered, networked, and nearly independent of livestock and crops grown in fields.

Choose your future food system. Will it be insects grown in urban farms delivered by robots? Or hamburgers made from cows outfitted with drones and sensors to improve their health and welfare? Or perhaps, once you've developed a healthy understanding of where food is and where it's going from the first five chapters, you'll be able to anticipate a universe we haven't yet thought of. The important thing to know is that you'll need to make some choices, and they may be more complicated and difficult than you imagine. Those who consume most of the food produced around the world will feel the ramifications of the choices we make now. Developing countries may be the first to feel the impact since they don't have an existing infrastructure to uproot and replace. They can begin now to implement some of these new technologies, to use data to determine the fastest and cheapest way to deliver fresh food to remote populations. Let's hope we get it right this time.

1 Our Food Supply Chain at a Glance

New Yorkers love their pizza slices. They eat them while running down some New York avenue on the way to work, or even while working, the sauce dripping down their wrists and into their sleeves. Slices became New Yorkers' preferred style of pizza because of the urban lifestyle of Manhattan, with its short lunch hours and mobile culture.

The New York pizza slice exists through a serendipitous combination of technological advancements and consumer lifestyles. When Italian immigrants came to New York in the early twentieth century, they brought their tomato sauce and flatbreads with them. But back then, the only tools for cooking those flatbreads were wood- and coal-fired ovens. At 900 degrees, they were—and still are—too hot to allow for the revered, reheated slices. Twenty years later, a new baking technology laid the framework for the New York slice as the arrival of natural gas deck ovens transformed the pizza trade. Now pizza bakers could use small ovens with low temperatures to reheat single slices, and in the decades following, New Yorkers adopted their slices.

The pizza slice perfectly conforms to the needs of New Yorkers who want a quick lunch they can eat on the run, with one hand. That simple slice of pizza can reveal the machinery behind the way our food supply chain works—and where it's going.

Modern food supply chains are complex systems, juggling many intermediate steps as raw ingredients transform and combine on their way to warehouses, transported by trucks, trains, barges, airplanes, ships, and even bicycles. Sometimes, food products are processed several times—cleaned, chopped, packaged, cooked, or combined into sauces—and all in different locations and by different middlemen. There's even a reverse food supply chain with its own logistics. Raw ingredients lurch, sprint, crawl, wait, and gather through a series of transformations called "farm to plate." The "to" is what makes feeding cities possible.

The story behind how our global food system evolved could fill several books. The history of agriculture alone deserves a deep dive since it gives us an idea of how far we've come in terms of how much we can grow on a single acre of land. But in this book, the story about the middle part—the supply chain and its path from farm to plate—is our hero. Confronting all sorts of monsters and enemies, that chain of events somehow manages to get us fed, more or less, every day. So before we dig into our pizza, let's define what we mean when we talk about food supply chains and logistics and take a brief look at how they developed into the system that fills our plates today.

The Evolution of Chain Logic

Food supply chains consist of a series of linked activities that occur while moving food from producers to consumers. These activities thrive on logistics. "Logistics" comes from the Greek word *logistik*, which means the art of planning for the purpose of moving goods and the related organization and equipment. It also relates to a French term, *logistique*, used by Antoine Henri de Jomini to describe the "practical art" of moving armies in *The Art of War* (1838). Jomini defined a commissariat as the coordinating center of an army's food supply. He thought of food as an essential fuel for military strategy and argued that a deficit in an army's food supply would lead to defeat in the field.

In that spirit, Jomini laid out the rules for keeping armies fed around supply depots that drew upon the resources of invaded regions. He believed an army would take about a month to occupy a region based upon that region's ability to feed it.[1] So beyond just moving stuff from point A to B, a logistics-based supply chain uses strategy, optimization, operations management, and quantified performance measurements. Today military and government research projects continue to develop logistics for feeding armies, and the innovations that originate in their labs often find their way to our grocery store shelves—energy bars, for example—or at least our camping supply stores, where we find freeze-dried meals that resemble military Meals-Ready-to-Eat or snacks originally created for NASA's space station.

During the late nineteenth and early twentieth centuries, the newly developed idea of scientific management led to practices that optimized workflow by carefully measuring and maximizing the use of time, labor, and standardized parts and practices while eliminating waste. Frederick Winslow Taylor, an early twentieth-century mechanical engineer, led the movement, and "Taylorism," as his theory was called, led to further improvements in the production and transportation of products from factory to consumer. The idea of optimization became quantifiable, and we began to scientifically optimize the time and distance between farms and plates. When computers arrived during the 1950s and 1960s, the idea of logical, rational workflows got an extra push through the acceleration of data processing, followed by the development of computer-based forecasting and materials planning systems. MIT scientist Jay Forrester led the research that later benefitted food processors and manufacturers to improve workflow. It wasn't until the 1980s, however, that supply chain management emerged, leading to supply chain centers in academic institutions. Food logistics acquired its own professional organizations, conferences, and academic departments. Automation joined with scale (large, centralized operations) to produce the global food supply system we see today.

During the same period, the late nineteenth and twentieth centuries, the development of ice manufacturing and refrigeration led to what is now called the "cold chain." The food supply chain differs from other supply chains in its requirement for careful temperature control. Entrepreneurs such as Augustus Swift revolutionized the meat supply chain by utilizing refrigerated rail cars and vertically integrating all aspects of meat production.

The arrival of railroads and shipping containers contributed two of the most significant changes in the food supply chain. Railroads began to move food across long distances beginning in the mid-nineteenth century, and shipping containers, developed by Malcom McLean during the 1950s and 1960s, transformed how food moved on ships, trucks, and trains. The integration of these transport networks eventually became our international, intermodal food distribution network.

With these new technologies, the industrialization of our food supply gained momentum and became global. Starting in the nineteenth century, farms and food processing companies grew in size. By the end of the 1800s, companies such as Unilever, General Mills, Nestlé, and Campbell's Soup Company represented the emergence of what we now call "Big Food." Back then size was the optimizer. Centralized facilities and aggregated activities enabled more food to be produced at lower costs.

Throughout this period, machinery gained ascendancy over humans as productivity became the objective. Henry Ford discovered that by using assembly lines he could mass-produce automobiles. Food companies adopted assembly line production practices and industrialized our food system. By World War II, the world's food system had gained more technology and logistics knowledge as a result of the necessities of warfare. Those assembly lines moved faster and produced food manufactured with more ingredients from laboratories than from the soil. We had become experts in producing food at scale with logistics and supply chains to match. The combination of size and scale with industrialization through the use of science and technology has given the world record-breaking food production at lower costs. Now all we need to do is to distribute all that food while making it more nutritious, maintaining freshness, and increasing access to consumers at all income levels while minimizing waste and any harmful impact to the environment, including humans. We're on the right path to solving for all this, but not without some unintended consequences. We don't really know yet how food, tech, and humans will accommodate each other. What do we know is that by keeping our eyes on four key ingredients that enable our food supply chain to operate today, we will increase our chances for success.

Four Ingredients That Keep Food Moving

Unlike many consumer products (such as electronics), food is fragile, emotional, cultural, and apt to expire on the way to our plates. Tacos aren't TVs. Scale and automation have gotten us fed so far, but not without assists from other interrelated ingredients. These are reliability, trust, adaptability, and technology.

The path we imagine our food takes to get to our plates is very often different from the real story. Our nonprofit organization in Austin, Texas, Food+City, tells stories of how the food supply chain works in a small magazine that often contains a road map for all the ingredients in a recipe or a simple food item, such as pizza. Turns out, it's never really a simple road map. It's full of logjams, detours, and dead ends. And those maps point to the four essential ingredients that keep our food flowing to our plates, illustrating how reliability, trust, technology, and adaptability overcome these obstacles.

These four ingredients are evident in all the stories in this book, and they will drive the design for our future food supply chains and distribution networks.

After visiting cities all over the world to learn about how food supply chains work for the simplest meals, I discovered that no matter how simple or sophisticated the supply chain, every link required our four ingredients in service of one common goal: to transport food from farm to table quickly, inexpensively, and sustainably while ensuring food safety. These ingredients enable our food to move from producer to consumer and interact in ways that optimize the system that delivers our food to our tables. Simple menu items can reveal how those who work in the supply chain business optimize a complex system by leveraging these ingredients.

Reliability

Logistics experts in every part of our food supply chain strive for consistency and reliability. Reliability is requisite because consumers expect some degree of consistency in products they consume. They expect price comparisons based on comparable characteristics: a kilo of walnuts should contain walnuts of consistent size, texture, and taste; and those few slightly brown bananas hidden at the bottom of the fruit basket will probably move to the waste bin. A reliable supply chain allows for consistent pricing and quality, which helps meet consumer expectations and minimize food waste. Commuters who head to Joe's pizza shop won't pay twenty dollars a slice, nor will they eat a Margherita slice that has a rubbery crust one day and a perfectly crisp crust the next. And that slice had better be the same size day after day.

Reliability and consistency dovetail with predictability. Procurement managers expect food deliveries to show up at their loading docks on schedule. Air cargo brokers need that fresh Alaskan salmon to be ready and sufficiently packed for planned flight schedules. Spontaneity doesn't cohabit with reliability much, and when it happens, it costs. When a food supply chain is reliable, it can minimize the risks and waste involved in delivering food to cities.

Joe's pizza provides a rich landscape for an exploration of our food supply chain. Grain, oil, meat, vegetables, and cheese converge on one menu item, offering stories of how multiple ingredients travel through the supply chain. The late Salvatore Riggio opened Pizza Suprema, a shop located just outside Madison Square Garden, in 1964. Now his wife, Maria, and their son, Joe, operate the shop, delivering hot slices to commuters who spill out of Penn Station.

I visited with Joe and Maria, meeting them one lunch hour as they sat working through invoices and other paperwork in a corner booth at the back of their pizza shop. Maria is petite, bright, and alert. Her eyes constantly scan the shop, signaling her wait staff to clear used plates and glasses and watching for napkins left behind by hurried lunchtime customers. Joe is built like a wrestler—in fact, he does wrestle, but only as a hobby. Now he's a family man, returning to the family business.

Both Joe and Maria are meticulous in the ways they choose to optimize their business. Before our pizza begins its journey to Joe's shop, he has to order the ingredients through a process called procurement. He decides what to purchase, whom to purchase it from, and at what price. If he's lucky and smart, he can keep just the right amount of pizza ingredients moving in the supply chain without waste and added expense. If he isn't so smart and fails to optimize his operations, moldy cheese piles up in warehouses and coolers, and those Penn Station commuters move on to Joe's competitors. Technologies, from warehouse management systems that include artificial intelligence for predictive inventory supplies to scanning and tracking tools that help manage shipments of ingredients, play into Joe's ability to sustain his business for all these years in New York City's very competitive food service industry.

Sourcing, as procurement is often called, can be local or global and draws upon technology, trust, and reliability. Joe buys his flour from General Mills, grown in North Dakota and milled in Buffalo, New York. The flour, called All Trumps 50111, is enriched with potassium, iron, potassium bromate, thiamin mononitrate, riboflavin, and folic acid, and it is a blend of wheat and malted barley flour. It's perfect for pizza, and it utilizes individual supply chains for all those enrichments. He gets pecorino cheese from Italy and mozzarella cheese from Wisconsin. His Stanislaus tomatoes come from California through a foodservice distributor, probably Sysco. Having multiple sources for an ingredient that's critical to his operation can lower risks and costs, but it adds complexity to tracking and food safety verification. And that's where trust comes in.

Trust

Trust comes with experience, as we learn from our own friendships. Food suppliers rely on the transit of assets and funds in exchange for products humans consume. Relationships, as with many business exchanges, are critical when it comes to food, since one bad apple could kill someone. Not only is food safety a requirement for the supply chain to operate successfully, but the delivery of quality and quantity across the globe is also much easier and more efficient when you know whom you're dealing with.

Sometimes trust will even trump convenience or price. One sesame seed buyer in Istanbul, Turkey, buys his seeds from Nigeria—from a man he has done business with for more than twenty years—rather than buy seeds from an unknown producer in his own country. And Mustafa, the owner of a fish and chips shop on Farringdon Street in London, depends upon close ties in the Turkish immigrant fish and chips community for all his supplies. He's not alone—many of the fish and chips shops I visited in the UK rely on Turkish suppliers for ingredients and equipment, since the trust among Turkish business owners runs deep and allows transactions to flow smoothly—often based on just a handshake.

Fortunately for Joe, years of working in the pizza business has also built relationships that run deep. Trusted networks of suppliers come from years of trading employees, stepping in for one another when problems arise, keeping secrets, and obeying the rules of credit and other financial transactions.

Joe gets his ingredients using the operation of food supply chains we've had for decades. He may decide to purchase cheese at a higher price from a local farmer because he wants to support local businesses. He may also decide to buy cheese from Italy at a higher price because Italy is the only source of that particular cheese; or, he may choose to purchase cheese thousands of miles away at a lower cost because the product he sells is price sensitive. Joe trusts his suppliers, and his customers trust that he will find the best ingredients at the best cost so that their pizzas will continue to be safe, tasteful, and affordable. The people sourcing our food rely on those trusted relationships that determine the resiliency of the supply chain. Our food supply chain will continue to rely on trusted relationships between farmers and buyers and between product companies and processors.

If the four ingredients (principles, not the kind Joe puts in his pizzas) are important to keep our food moving along the supply chain under regular conditions, they become absolutely critical when things go wrong. During my visit to Pizza Suprema, we talked about Hurricane Sandy, which hit New York City in 2012, disrupting everything. The shop closed for four days, limited mostly by the lack of power. For the pizza man, the first thing to go wrong in a power outage is the cheese inventory. Flour, canned tomatoes, spices, and olive oil can last for weeks. But cheese goes bad in days—even four days.

To make matters worse, Joe's cheese supplier, Grande, couldn't get its trucks to his shop because of road closures and traffic. Of course, even if the trucks could've gotten through, the lack of power would have spoiled the shipments. Keeping the shop running would require another of our key ingredients: adaptability. So Joe called up his pizza business friend in Brooklyn, who still had power, and he got some shredded cheese to replace the cheese normally delivered from his supplier in Wisconsin. That adaptability is an example of the flexibility and durability that allows the supply chain to get food to our plates in spite of interruptions and breakdowns. By acquiring the cheese from his Brooklyn friend, Joe was able to resume his business in four days, which is a miracle considering that some New Yorkers were still, in 2013, not back to business as usual.

Even "business as usual" belies the complications of delivering a simple menu item and illustrates how those four ingredients operate to keep the supply chain moving. There's a deli in Austin that makes a ridiculously delicious club sandwich. The store in Austin is part of Jason's Deli, a chain of 275 delis located in 28 states. A few years ago, a group of students at the University of Texas at Austin worked with Food+City to track down the supply chain for the sandwich and found that the ingredients traveled to its delis from several countries, including Finland.

Jason's Deli club sandwich consists of bread, ham, Swiss and cheddar cheeses, bacon, lettuce, and tomatoes, but each ingredient in the sandwich includes micro-ingredients, just like the flour General Mills makes for Joe's pizza. The students found that the bread alone had its own complex path from wheat field to deli, and Jason's story is similar to the stories of bread produced in other countries. Wheat farmers in Kansas grew the wheat, which was sent by rail to a mill that distributed the ground wheat to bakeries. Other ingredients, such as water, yeast, flaxseed, wheat gluten, and sugar, also found their way to the bakeries. The flaxseed came from Nebraska, the wheat gluten from Poland, and the sugar from sugar cane grown in Georgia and Louisiana. The flow of all these micro-ingredients needed to converge at a bakery that produced the bread. Then the bread would travel onward through a distribution system that eventually landed in a single Jason's Deli location for assembly into a sandwich. The mustard, too, contained micro-ingredients—including mustard seeds, oil, and salt— and the theme continued across every part of the sandwich. Each ingredient consisted of several micro-ingredients, each micro-ingredient had its own supply chain, and if just one of those chains broke down, the whole sandwich would have to be reconsidered. Fortunately, the supply chain is incredibly adaptable, both positively and negatively, for finding substitutions and adulterations.

Adaptability

Jason's supply chain requires sublime adaptability, reliability, trust, and technology to operate successfully. If one rail car gets sidetracked by a snowstorm, the wheat will mold. Or if longshoremen decide to strike at Houston's port, the wheat gluten from Poland and the cheese from Finland won't be able to enter the United States through trusted brokers.

Even when our four key ingredients are present, they don't always lead to success. Failure to deliver food happens. The unobstructed, easy flow of the supply chain is the aim of everyone in the global food system. If we could achieve our goal, we'd grow exactly enough healthy food to exactly match the individual demand of all consumers, so food waste would cease to exist. The reason this hasn't yet been achieved is because of friction within the machinery of the food supply chain. Friction points are points that cause the supply chain to halt, break, leak, or misdirect our food. Understanding these friction points may help us eliminate, or at least lubricate them.

Friction points include traffic and urban congestion, broken equipment, labor strikes, decaying transportation networks (including potholes in roads), wars, theft, electrical outages, climate changes, and trade sanctions. Any one of these conditions puts pressure on the supply chain to adapt and to re-create reliability.

The ability of the supply chain to adapt is critical to overcoming many of these friction points: Derailed trains? Trucks might suffice. Ports closed? Ships may enter through alternative ports and their cargo could travel to their original destinations in trucks. The system has to adapt, and the effort to supply food with some order of reliability enables the system to minimize waste, maintain quality, and keep costs down. Adaptability is one of the supreme ingredients of our food supply chain, and we see it in action every day. It modulates both friction and flow within the system as changes occur throughout the pathway from farm to plate.

It's not just the "logistical" issues that fuel the need for adaptability. As consumers, we constantly create other friction points that require food providers to adjust the way the supply chain works at a moment's notice. Changes in our behavior as consumers initiate a ripple effect throughout the chain as it adapts in order to optimize. We reject certain food items such as gluten or peanuts, or we embrace others such as coconut water and kale, creating wild oscillations in sourcing, production, and processing. But as we know that food relies on natural cycles of germination, weather, and biological systems, quick adaptations are hardly the norm. And at the same time, our preferences for improved labor and animal welfare practices cause food producers to scramble for new suppliers.

Consider the movements to remove antibiotics from meat, raise chickens in cage-free environments, consume less meat and more plants, and eat organic or locally grown food. An agile supply chain prides itself on its adaptability. For example, if insect flour became the latest food ingredient to improve health, it would require a quick response to fill its supply chain since the requirements for the raw material may be unique and unanticipated, requiring new storage and transport solutions

Beyond mercurial tastes, other changes in consumer behavior—whether based upon new health data, concerns about the environment, or prices—all cause the food supply chain to adapt. When the general public deemed genetically modified organisms (GMO) unhealthy in spite of established research to the contrary, the supply chain had to find new sources and methods for segregating the non-GMO from the GMO ingredients and meeting the increased demand for organic food production. At Whole Foods' warehouses, organic produce must be stored above the nonorganic produce to prevent any contamination.

This means that grain storage and handling facilities will also have to be segregated, potentially creating pressure for capacity. This need for separation may, in the long run, lead to more direct shipping without any stops for consolidation. In the short term, additional costs and delays may arise, as each supply chain needs testing and verification to ensure no contamination has occurred.

Demographic change, another growing friction point in the food supply chain, is on the rise due to climate changes and conflict around the world. Increasing wealth in developing countries such as those in Asia and South America has created larger middle-class populations that demand high-end, sophisticated brands and products. Meat consumption has historically been an indicator of social status. A country's improvement in its standard of living is typically matched with an increase in meat consumption. Despite concerns about animal welfare and the environmental impact of livestock operations, meat consumption is on the rise worldwide.[2]

Changes in the way labor markets operate also affect the flow of food—particularly elimination of the middleman. In the coffee business, Fair Trade coffee emerged as a way for small producers to sell directly to companies in countries where coffee is consumed, enabling coffee farmers to receive a larger share of profits.

As the sheer variety of foods on supermarket shelves continues to grow, the proliferation of what retailers call SKUs, Stock Keeping Units, is a challenge for any retailer. Each SKU represents a product, and everyone up and down the supply chain is tracking, separating, and managing more and more products. We want choices, and we have them: in the last five years, the number of SKUs in the grocery business increased by 50 percent, yet supply chains are still trying to keep up with consumer demands for these new products.[3]

We, in the developed world, have come to expect choices and variety in what we eat. These demands have only increased in complexity to bring us where we are today: pivoting away from our traditional food supply chains to a new, disintermediated, personal, localized food supply chain. And some big food companies attempt to appear as small companies by featuring an artisanal producer and sustainable practices. The boundaries between big food companies and small producers will eventually erode as we begin to see more technology and online sales flatten our sourcing landscape in much the same way as online markets appear place-less, inhabiting a digital world.

As the number of products proliferates and we advocate for local food, our supply chain finds ways to adapt. For example, the food industry has tried to adapt during the recent economic period of slow growth and low interest rates by consolidating in order to deliver shareholder value. Food companies have been merging or acquiring other companies. JBS S.A., Kraft, and ABInBev (the world's largest brewer) are examples of food companies that have followed this strategy. As a result, the number of companies that produce and deliver food has been dwindling. However, this consolidation makes the supply chain more vulnerable through the loss of redundancy and diversity. And that vulnerability causes the current move toward disaggregation of the industry into smaller, distributed food companies that strive to be more accommodating, flexible, and responsible to consumers who want specialized products.

Joining changes in consumer behavior that require an adaptable food supply chain are changes in weather and climate, including natural disasters like Hurricane Sandy. During the winter of 2013 and 2014, cold temperatures in the United States increased the need for railroads to deliver tanker cars of crude oil to heat areas with frigid temperatures in a winter that lasted longer than expected. Hopper cars—railroad cars that contain prairie or seed corn—were replaced by tanker cars, thus delaying the arrival of corn for planting. As a result, crops germinated later and harvests were delayed, sending corn into the supply chain later in the season. To complicate matters even more, corn producers had a record harvest in 2013, but the railroads were so busy delivering oil and coal that there weren't enough trains to move the harvest through the supply chain, creating backlogs in areas that eventually ran out of storage capacity in grain elevators. Three months went by as farmers were stuck holding onto grain that couldn't find rail cars. Since there was less rail capacity, prices for shipping grain rose, and farmers, already operating on thin margins, had to pay more to ship what they could. In the end, the supply chain adapted by building more storage capacity and shipping corn by truck rather than by rail.[4] This adaptability does come at a cost when the supply chain continues to change, continually adding to the ongoing costs of adaptations.

Any change in any one of part of the supply chain causes a ripple throughout the supply chain and logistics plan. For example, when powdered milk and soluble coffee became possible, new supply chains emerged to accommodate those new ingredients. And the ripples of that "butterfly effect" pass through state and national boundaries. One change in Bangladesh causes another in a Washington seaport. A discovery of slave labor in a coffee plantation in West Africa can result in a dislocation of dock labor, decline in warehouse capacity, and increase in coffee prices—not to mention the disappearance of beans from your barista's roaster.

Even a change in currency rates, like the recent strength of the US dollar, can cause the supply chain to flex toward other sources of food. These changes may be long term or short and seasonal. Some of the flexing is predictable based on seasonal surges. The food supply chain has been adapting at ever-increasing speeds these days as the increase in the demand for organic food has outpaced the supply of organic farmers.[5]

Technology

In many cases, trust, reliability, and adaptability rely on technology. Technology has contributed to safer food, a greater choice of ingredients in our diet, and new transportation infrastructures. Since Jethro Tull invented the seed drill and the impactful steam and combustion engines came into wide use, food has never been so widely and quickly distributed. Now, new technology is affecting the food supply chain by changing the way we order, purchase, process, store, transport, and produce our food. The topology or framework of the technologies that have led to automation and scale, big and centralized food distribution, will have the biggest impact on our future food system. The move from a centralized, global food system to a distributed, more localized food system will depend upon technological innovations that will make all that data and all that connectivity work on behalf of a better, healthier, and more vibrant—and maybe even more human—food system.

But there's a dark side to all these technological improvements. Viewers of the Netflix series *Black Mirror* are familiar with all the ways technology can be deployed for sinister purposes, and our global food supply is no exception. In 2017, Jason's Deli confirmed a data breach that revealed at least two million customer credit card numbers. While this wasn't a hack that contaminated Jason's food supply chain, breaches in the security and safety of our food system could significantly threaten public health.

We'll cover the dark side throughout this book, but this is just an example of how some of the four ingredients—technology, reliability, adaptability, and trust—can backfire, subverting their potential for optimization. But when used in a positive way, these ingredients keep our food flowing day after day. And since time is the enemy of food quality, every member of the supply chain must leverage those four ingredients to put fresh, affordable food on consumers' tables.

As we've seen, Jason and Joe both benefit from the development of logistics and supply chain technology. The opportunity to optimize is a result of mature societies and technology. Societies that still rely on subsistence farming are looking for a way—any way—to get surplus food from their fields to the market.

Optimization is both an art and a science, but in the end, both art and science work together in search of the best or most optimal way to move food that costs less, preserves or improves quality, minimizes environmental impact, creates jobs that create wealth and satisfaction, and offers the maximum amount of healthful nutrition to everyone—human and nonhuman. This rationalization, an attempt to make sense of each activity in the supply chain, strives to optimize the path from farm to plate.

While the idea of optimization is the goal of food logistics, we haven't reached peak optimization, and even barring friction-producing events like the ones we've discussed, everyday shortcomings in our food system lead to wasted food, time, and resources. The current outcry over the amount of food waste we produce is a sign of a lack of optimization. We may find instances, and they abound, where the supply chains appear completely suboptimal. But often, what seems optimal to us (exclusive focus on locally grown, organic produce, for example) is not, and the common practices that make perfect sense to the food-supply pros seem ludicrous to the hungry consumers. Circuitous routes that take tomatoes from Mexico to China and back to the United States seem inconsistent with optimization. But they are optimized, mostly, because of paradoxes that are invisible to the consumer. A paradox results when fishermen in New England send tuna to Japan to a market where sushi buyers from Boston purchase the same tuna to fly it back to their customers in New England. We'll see examples of these paradoxes throughout this book. Watch for them, since they suggest how adaptable our supply chains are and offer insights about where we might reimagine how we can move food. And they also illustrate how our food supply chain uses optimization for someone's advantage. We may think the path of those fish is suboptimal, but someone in the sushi supply chain thinks it's the best option, delivering the best product at the best price.

If size and industrialization were the old optimizers, today's optimizers include computers and connectivity. Much like centralized computing has given way to distributed, personal computing, the behemoths on the food scene are making way for smaller, distributed, more localized, and more personalized production and delivery techniques. The new digital and connected optimizers include applications for tracking, tracing, packaging, and transporting food. They are transforming how we will eat in the future and are rearranging our relationship with our food. The Internet of Things (IoT) is becoming the Internet of Food (IoF) as we connect food to digital data networks with more transparency. Cloud-based food, food on demand, and possibly even printed or lab fabricated food will become possibilities when nutrition flows as data through interconnected data highways. We can see this shift occurring in the way the food supply chain adapts to weather, demographics, conflicts, and scarcity. Faster data networks will enable faster, more distributed responses to these sourcing changes, and they will take us to a new level of optimization.

Technology is the big ingredient that will drive our food system forward. Big Data accelerates and improves reliability and adaptability, and new devices such as drones and scanners take trust to a new level. Future adaptations will include the gradual personalization of food as producers react to consumer behavior designed by consumers' own health data. New sources of protein, such as lab meat made from plants or cells, will spark new supply chains for plant material and cells while impacting the demand cycle for animal-based protein. The power of big data combined with connectivity will affect the entire food supply chain, from production to transportation and distribution.

Big food data and the Internet of Food will accelerate the move of local, fresh food to our growing urban populations. Consumers will demand that these networks operate faster, pointing to the need for innovations that shorten the time to develop new sourcing, invent new ingredients, and change the labor component within the supply chain. If robots take over the food-processing industry, manufacturers may not need to concern themselves with improving human labor practices. But they will need to deal with the sea change in their workforces and workplaces.

In the future, disruptions in the food supply chain will be mitigated by new digital routing software that integrates artificial intelligence (AI). The lack of locomotives required to move food during seasonal shifts could lead to the Uber model for locomotive or rail car sharing. This is happening in the trucking business. Convoy Logistics, one of many third-party logistics companies, úses the latest digital tools to fill truckloads and trace shipments. If railroads could overcome their long-held resistance to automation, they could use data networks to anticipate uneven demand for trains and locomotives and move assets into place to fill the gaps. Some railroad companies are starting these upgrades, but it will take time until they move from iron-based thinking to cloud-based thinking. Many of the computer systems used by railroad companies are old and outdated, reliant on centralized computing rather than distributed networks. New rail systems are integrating new technology, such as the Silk Road project that will connect China with Europe. DHL has contracted with the Latvian Railways to build high-speed rail services, promising guaranteed transit times and integrated customs processing and tracking as food cargo passes between all the countries along the route.[6] These new routes will move faster without the baggage of union bargaining and outdated infrastructures that would need removal or expensive retrofitting.

Another dynamic that provides opportunities for technology to optimize the food supply chain is demographic change, as people take their food culture and practices with them when they move from place to place. Immigrants from Libya, Syria, and Sudan arrived in Western European countries demanding their native ingredients prepared according to their own cultural practices. France now has a growing Halal meat-processing center within Rungis, the large wholesale food market outside Paris. Personalized food, based on genetic databases and AI, will enable these demographic migrations and shifting communities to bring their personal food preferences along with them, maybe through a facial recognition tool.

Severe disruptions caused by conflicts, both natural and unnatural, will draw upon the new Internet of Food. Food logisticians and suppliers often work together to plan scenarios that model disruptions so they can create contingency plans they hope they never need. These models will be more adaptive, real-time, and able to leverage quantum computers to model nuanced scenarios. Sysco and the American Red Cross now partner for the purpose of creating disaster plans for food distribution. But they may soon integrate virtual reality (VR) and augmented reality (AR) in dynamic training and modeling for disaster training. More robust networks and infrastructures will need to accompany these response teams in remote and underdeveloped regions. Without a basic road network and a power grid, emergency food supplies don't get far. A lack of power won't get you a bowl of rice. Hybrid networks may close the gap and include balloons along with drones for aid package distribution.

Agile adaption to changes in consumer behavior requires suppliers to find alternative sources in fairly short timeframes. Consumers react to information about food suppliers, production practices, and nutrition, and they can switch buying practices in significant ways. As the speed of information transmission increases, consumers are learning more and more about food, nutrition, labor practices, prices, and new foods.

However, those who are convinced that food supply chains are on the verge of revolutionary transformation often overlook one thing—the fact that, unlike TVs, tomatoes and other food ingredients perish. Tomatoes rot if left alone for too long, apples bruise and become untenable, spoiled eggs can kill a consumer, and just the appearance of imperfection can put a product into the waste bin. Trust in the food supply chain isn't optional. Sure, trust can be created through specious methods, but food depends upon trusting relationships among everyone in the chain, from producers to consumers. If there's a flutter in trust, the chain collapses. Building that trust takes time, and even though we're familiar with rating systems and crowd-sourced feedback, in the end, a human is at the end of every trusted relationship. The thing about food and our future is that humans have been at the center of our food system since the beginning of time, but now we're about to remove humans from our food system faster and more completely than ever before. Just what that means is unclear. We have some guesses: no more immigrant labor picking heads of lettuce, more choices for how we want our food delivered, and more fresh food grown locally. But what about us?

As our food supply chain becomes more and more automated, digital, connected, and smart, it will be held to a higher standard than TVs. No offense to the television industry, but food is fragile, and so is our relationship with it. Humanity is embedded in the very meaning of food, its purpose, and its consumption. You can put a 3-D printed pizza on the table, but the humans will swarm around it with suspicion, and the removal of the human baker twirling a pie overhead, puffs of flour swirling in sympathy, may have unintended consequences. It's too early to grasp the full meaning of food tech, as we commonly call this digital convergence of art and science.

How will we find that equipoise of convenience and our thirst for transparency and trust? Maybe we'll view tacos more like TVs. Or maybe we'll protest the production of our food by engineers instead of dirt farmers. Either way, it's too early to predict the future of food with any accuracy at a moment when new applications of technology are appearing every day in a climate of constant change.

2 Food Roots

A group of friends in Austin recently gathered around the dining table to share a meal. As consummate meat eaters, these Texans don't mess around when it comes to their BBQ. But this time, they confronted a "clean" burger, one made out of plants, not a Texas Angus. Stubborn by nature, but somewhat curious, they took their first bites. After a pause, they eventually agreed: "Not bad . . . pretty good . . . I could eat this if I had to."

Engineers in a California lab who made that burger possible had performed a miracle. Called Impossible Foods, the company managed to make a burger in a lab without even a wink in the direction of a cow. Are we now watching as the makeup of the food on our plate becomes unrecognizable? Just because it fits between two hamburger buns, is it meat? And is that white liquid you poured over your cereal milk, or something else? And if so, what happens to all those Texas Angus? And how will these new foods impact the broader food supply chain? If we all drink milk made from almonds, how will we reconcile the dairy substitute's dependence upon water in California, where water is a scarce commodity? In spite of our desire for simple, clean ingredients, are we really leaning toward greater complexity?

It's Personal

The connection between what we eat and where it comes from has become a global obsession. It's either Michael Pollan or Dan Barber or the too-affable server in a local restaurant that tells us where our food comes from these days. It's not as if we never wanted to know before—we did. We just weren't interested in every morally and ethically laden detail about our food's routes from its roots to our dining rooms.

Why this obsession, and what does this story have to do with where our food system is going next? Mostly, the motive behind this prevalent curiosity is about trust, one of our four ingredients mentioned in chapter 1. Our earliest ancestors raised, grew, harvested, and prepared their food themselves, so there was never a question as to where it came from or how it was prepared. But the moment we invited others to process, pack, and store our food, we lost track of what happens between farms and our plates. Mostly, we lost trust in the system as the invisibles crept between the farmer and us. We imagined the worst, and in some cases the worst was happening: animals were abused, crops were sprayed with toxic chemicals, and somehow our food became less nutritious and flavorful. Now we want to gain back the trust for those who make our food. After all, food is personal. In some cases, intimate. At its most extreme, knowing more about our food can be a matter of life and death.

Our Complicated Relationship with Our Plates

This is where the optimizers collide with the murky and intangible aspects of our food system. Our food evokes emotional responses tied to our own origins. While the previous chapter explained how optimization of the food supply chain is rooted in quantifiable, measurable goals, this chapter will add to the irrational side of the global food supply chain. Yes, there are still a lot of optimized and measurable aspects to our food production system, but the system is highly influenced by some of our feelings about people and places. That's what makes food logistics so complicated. And as University of Texas at Austin psychologist Dr. Art Markman points out, we humans really shy away from understanding complex systems.

This collision between optimization and the more social and cultural meanings of food means that humans won't leave our food supply chain quietly. They may not entirely give up their participation in the making and distributing of our food, in spite of all the rational, quantifiable, optimal reasons for leaving the system to the machines that will eventually know more than we do. Leaving the field for computers isn't a slam dunk. Or is it? What makes the engineering of our food supply chain so problematic? Ask Natalia.

In 2013, I visited a piroshky shop in Moscow and met the owner, Natalia. She was as excited about her new shop as any entrepreneur and took me on a tour of her bakery, which was located in an abandoned aircraft factory. She spent her childhood cooking pastries with her grandmother and eventually became an engineer, working on space acoustics equipment transmitters. Natalia remembers the smell of sweet, baked pastries in the mornings as the piroshkies emerged from a long night in the oven.

After four years of building her business, she now manages a team who begins their ritual baking process during the early morning hours and supplies most of the businesses in the surrounding areas. As she shared one of her fresh piroshkies with me over a cup of steaming, fragrant tea, she described how she felt about her business. To Natalia, the piroshky business evoked a sense of belonging to a larger community. It also provided her the means to share her love of childhood piroshkies. All of these associations were baked into her pies.

Just as Natalia was developing a plan to launch her business in the United States, trade sanctions between the West and Russia closed down any aspirations for an expansion outside of Russia. Russia became the target of trade sanctions as a result of its actions in the Ukraine. Some of Moscow's restaurants could no longer get European cheeses, among other items. And Natalia wouldn't be able to seek out the European butter that made her piroshkies so light and flakey.

Playing on a surge of nationalism, President Vladimir Putin made a campaign out of Russia becoming independent of outside food, including European butter. Russians began sporting T-shirts emblazoned with "Eat Russian!" Food sourcing can become part of a political campaign and be a powerful symbol of national and ethnic identity. There is nothing rational per se about buying Russian butter and cheese for her piroshkies, but Natalia is Russian after all, and supporting the growth of a Russian butter and cheese maker would bring together several emotional connections among food, identity, politics, and local pride. One Russian cheese maker has named one of his cows "Sanctions" in honor of the boost those restrictions gave his business.[1]

The emotional connection we have with our food, whether bound by politics or national and ethnic identity, is common and evident in the Texan obsession with BBQ, the Japanese with sushi, the Australian with Vegemite, and the British with fish and chips. You can find enthusiasts who will go to the ends of the earth to evangelize their beloved food. Our identity, not to mention our survival, is connected to our food, as evidenced by those Texans who long for Longhorns. This makes optimization unreasonably complicated, because it means we have a built-in conflict between how we want our food system to function and how we allow it to function in order to balance this tension between optimal sourcing (what's rational, measurable, and cost effective) and irrational sourcing (what's convenient, popular, or expedient).

Food in Its Place

Geography, the environment, politics, economics, and technology influenced who grew our food and where they grew it. As soon as urban landscapes began to industrialize and people began to leave farms for jobs in cities during the eighteenth and nineteenth centuries, urban reformers began to think about the connection between food, cities, and geography. Urban reformers in Europe and the United States observed the shifts in urban landscapes and sought a redesign of the placement of food relative to cities. We've been curious about where and how our food is produced for a long time.

We used to live close to our food because most of us lived on the farms where it was produced. Eventually, we moved into cities for jobs and became accustomed to public markets and backyard gardens. Some of us kept our own pigs and chickens for a while as we brought our rural habits with us. But eventually, we began to rethink the connection between food and cities.

This movement of food from rural landscapes into urban landscapes, back out to rural landscapes, and now back to urban landscapes reflects our changing notions about who should produce our food and how. We send food out of cities when we want public sanitation and a removal of blood and animals from our modern life. We remove food production when land in our cities becomes too expensive for farming and requires too much space to feed everyone in the city. We bring it back into the city when land values can support the economies of scale and the revenues generated and costs saved by having food produced close to consumers. We have been a capricious world, pulling up our roots and moving food away and closer, depending upon economics, politics, and geography.

One of the first cities to feel this tension over where food should live was London. During the nineteenth century, London was gathering in rural populations as the Industrial Revolution was transforming labor from handwork to machine work, and Londoners watched with both horror and fascination. The fascinated filled books and journals with observations and statistics that depicted a modern London with all its improvements. But as London led the industrialization and modern urbanization of cities, it also represented a rethinking of the relative locations of food and cities that transformed urban landscapes around the world.

The key issues in the battle to remove the world's largest live cattle market, Smithfield Market, from the middle of London to the suburb of Islington were traffic congestion, public health, land values, and the arrival of new technology. Pressure from these modern developments pushed food outside the city where the environment was more salubrious, land values were lower, and traffic congestion didn't impede food or people from reaching their destinations. By the mid-nineteenth century, urban landscapes everywhere were beginning to change, and urban reformers had begun to leave their marks in the form of modern ideas about how to mitigate the detritus left behind by the Industrial Revolution. Not everyone got a factory job, and the numbers of urban poor that suffered from malnutrition or died from cholera increased throughout the nineteenth century. Doctors hadn't yet made the scientific connection between urban sanitation and public health, and so food markets and butchers were blamed for the rise in urban deaths. Removing those activities that filled the rivers and streets with food detritus seemed a good move in order to improve public health. And making land occupied by food markets and food production available to developers was a way to increase rents and tax revenues. These pressures on urban landscapes continue today, but economics and consumers are shifting priorities, and some of the costs and benefits are following. Bringing food production and processing closer to consumers is a way to increase trust, and we may be willing to accept higher food costs as a tradeoff.

Beginning with the earliest battles over our food's roots, trust between consumers and producers of food was just one of the issues caught in the debate about where we live and where our food comes from. Technology is another force that reoriented food production and its relationship to cities. London's transport revolution brought railways into the urban landscape above and below ground and began to connect the countryside with the urban spaces. Railways increased land values in London and bridged greater distances along the food supply chain to hungry urban dwellers.

Cattle markets moved to the suburbs by the late nineteenth century, and railroads brought the meat from countryside slaughterhouses into the urban public markets.

Before transport technologies improved the movement of people and their food, rural sellers and shopkeepers who remained in small towns survived with fewer products and higher prices. The arrival of transport technologies that connected farms to cities during the eighteenth and nineteenth centuries was preceded by other technological advancements in agriculture that were the results of discoveries made during the Scientific Revolution of the sixteenth and seventeenth centuries. A gradual increase in food productivity followed and continues until the present day. Food became a commodity and joined coal and other high-volume products that enjoyed economies of scale. Sellers of food commodities had control of the market since consumers had no other options. The small-town shopkeeper lost his competitive advantage and eventually disappeared. With the increases in food production, there were good reasons for production to stay outside of cities where land costs were high and concerns about urban sanitation and public health remained. We see this cycle today, moving food and its related supply chain back and forth, toward urban centers and away from them.

Our industrialized food production system, based upon scale and automation until now, has also caused dislocations of both supply and demand. Making more food, and thus lowering the price and increasing its availability, has been good for society, but we've lost trust and transparency in the process. By the turn of the twentieth century, progressive thinkers everywhere began to challenge the rippling effects of industrialization and factories. Sinclair Lewis was outraged at the meatpacking industry in his book *The Jungle* (1909), published a few years after Rudyard Kipling provided a vivid description of Chicago slaughterhouses. In England, in an effort to reintroduce humans to their rural landscapes, the urban reformer Ebenezer Howard began designing cities that incorporated farms and launched the garden city movement in urban design.

Science and Technology: Friend or Foe?

Concern over unseen and unsavory food production practices continued to grow, and a new pushback emerged during the late 1950s that was a harbinger of the environmental movement of the 1970s. With the increased yields of agriculture had come concern about the impact of chemicals and intensive farming practices on the environment. Self-identified hippies and "back-to-the-landers" promoted organic farming, "health" food, and a return to grassroots agriculture as a solution. Still, however, during the 1950s and 1960s, scientists and agronomists like Norman Borlaug used technology such as hybridization to continue on the path toward increased yields, especially with wheat in developing countries. Art and science, the human and mechanical, were engaged in a contest for control of our food system.

The idea of genetically modifying food for nutritional and productivity purposes was central to these scientists' research. The Green Revolution, as Borlaug's work came to be identified with, introduced synthetic fertilizers, pesticides, and crop hybridization as tools of the new cultivators. An illustration of how words evolve to have entirely different meanings, "green" in today's culture excludes many of the practices introduced during the Green Revolution. What will "green" mean in a digital food system?

By the time World War II rolled around, cities were aware of the relationship between military conflicts and food security. Cities began developing plans for securing food supply chains in case they were cut off from food supplies. Their concerns continue today as cities develop food policies, promote green landscapes, and encourage local food production. We're once again rethinking the relationship of food and our cities, and this time we're thinking digital. Gradually, we're bringing food back into cities bit by bit, bite by byte, and, eventually, nibble by nibble.

So what changed that allowed the return of food markets and production back into the heart of our cities? Are there new developments that offset land values, public health issues, and the high costs of distributing food through urban space? Or will urban agriculture and farmers' markets eventually boomerang back out of the cities once again? Or is our emotional attachment to food overruling our desire for optimization?

Food and the City

The relationship between food and cities is a long story, and its ending is still not in sight. The association is emotional yet engineered, inextricable yet fluid. We want our food close to us, yet food production is a messy business that's costly and dependent upon scale. The placement of food in relation to the cities where we live affects its cost, safety, and environmental impact. Distance, geography, economics, and transportation infrastructure weigh in as food finds its place in our cities, and a sense of place related to food informs where and how our supply chains work.

Today, we label our preference for food grown nearby the "local food movement," and describing the return of food to our cities as a "movement" is particularly apt. Food logistics is all about movement. Self-conscious movement is an obsession of chefs these days. Menus tout local sources and take great pains to list all their suppliers. Chefs and grocery stores become storytellers, often including photos of the families who harvest their produce and maps that prove the proximity of the purveyors. During an interview with one of our star restaurant owners in Texas, I noticed a map on the wall that illustrated all the farms that provided ingredients to the chef. This story appears on menus, websites, and similar wall charts these days as chefs work to satisfy consumers' demands for locally sourced food.

While farmers should be encouraged as entrepreneurs and small business owners, they struggle to find the time to build and operate local businesses, connecting with customers like this chef. Two of our beloved local farms in Austin announced they were closed or dramatically downsized just this year. Farming is a 24/7 occupation, and giving up farm time to market produce is often impractical.

And the pain points for traditional, land-based food production are enormous. One of those Austin farms faced over $100K of storm damage from a winter storm. Crop insurance, subsidies, climate changes, government regulations and trade policies, labor, and . . . weeds. All of these friction points make food production in general more and more stressful and unsustainable. They are almost deal-breakers for the creation of a local food system.

Still, the pressure to get food from local producers is real, and it can have unintended consequences for everyone. Direct-to-consumer sales (the term the USDA uses to describe farmers' markets, the direct sales of food from farm to local chefs, and community-supported agriculture) aren't nearly as simple as they might sound. For the farmer, selling and delivering food to customers requires access to trucks (sometimes refrigerated trucks) and drivers. But these trucks are often partially filled, consuming energy for a high cost per calorie. Chefs like the one across the table from me that day are taking deliveries from up to thirty trucks a day, each with a locally produced ingredient. The expansive carbon footprint cannot be sustainable. But the customers don't see this side of the supply chain. They only see the distance between farms and tables. And distance is both a rational, measurable concept and one that's entirely in our heads.

What does "local" mean? For some, local means small, personal, human. Because food is both personal *and* produced by big food companies outside of our towns and cities, we often struggle to reconcile our sense of personal ethics with our perceptions of the institutions that manufacture our food. As a result, we tend to measure our feelings by the distance between the producers and our plates.

Local and global food systems are caught in a contest for jobs, nutrition, cultural identity, and environmental integrity. And this is not a new conundrum. As far back as the fourth century, observers noted that cities needed diversified sources of food in order to provide food security if trade was cut off or if local crops were infested or damaged by weather.

Food at Scale

Bigness has come to mean badness. Profit commandeering principles, people sacrificed for efficiency, truth traded for image. Coffee beans picked and dried by slave labor. Vanilla beans harvested by food mafias that sell on the black market. Smallness implies trust, humanity, and transparency in our minds. A family that farms in Vermont or a Nigerian goat farmer. And since humans don't work well with complex systems, the simple idea of "big is bad, small is good" sits in the sweet spot for most of us as an operating principle for choosing who we want to produce our food and where we want them to be relative to our cities. Those who distrust big food companies believe small farms are more transparent and trustworthy. And consumers who worry about food security feel that having food grown nearby is a wise strategy for cities that may be cut off from long-distance supply chains. These contentious perspectives of size sit in a landscape of space and distance. The big guys are far away, and the little guys are nearby, even if only in our imaginations. Hence the demand for local food.

Ethical sourcing, sustainable practices, and food justice are all concepts that imply that our food supply chain needs to be held accountable. So we lean into our food supply system, trying to see who is growing, processing, and shipping our food. In our collective minds, "ethical" has become synonymous with "local," and the sustainability of our global food supply chain is often cast in terms of distance.

The more complex, systematic way of looking at where our food comes from is found in such issues as the costs of shipping food over long distances. We consumers think that long distance travel for food is unsustainable, not to mention bad news for our tender tomatoes, which must be bred to withstand vibrating long-haul vehicles. It must cost more, damage the food, require chemicals to extend shelf life, and consume fossil fuels that end up polluting our environment. But is this really true? Are we trying to solve the right problems? And are these problems of real concern to those of us who eschew complexity? Can technology solve for bigness and create a food system that is transparent enough that we feel a close personal connection that's not measured in terms of miles or kilometers?

To understand the complex question of whether long or short food supply chains are better for us and the environment, we need to settle on a way to measure distance. After all, no one can agree on the definition of "local." Local in Texas is not local in Belgium. And where do we draw the line? Is food from Northern California considered "local" to Southern California? Since food is a perishable commodity, does a short trip to your plate make it fresher? Do the farm and its owner become part of our family if we can somehow "know" them by their proximity to our tables?

The USDA defines "local" as a measurable distance between food production and consumption that is four hundred miles or less.[2] Anything sourced from a longer distance would not be considered local. Of course, four hundred miles feels like five when you're in Texas, but in Rhode Island you can buy "local" food from any of the adjoining states. Keep in mind that the complexity and value of a food supply chain relates to how many intermediaries there are between a producer and consumer. So, it's not necessarily all about the measured distance between you and your food.

One big wrinkle for the local food movement is selection. Buying local can only support consumption of food that grows naturally in your community. The region that feeds a city or location is a foodshed, and the truth is, we may live in a foodshed with cranberry bogs instead of coffee plantations. Think of New York City's foodshed as a large circle that radiates from the city into Maryland in the south and up to Boston in the northeast.[3] All the producers within that region are considered to be part of the New York City foodshed, where oyster beds, apple orchards, and maple syrup all live together. Urban food systems policy planners are continually looking at production within a foodshed, often requiring that a certain amount of available food in the city or state come from within that foodshed or providing financial incentives to local farmers.[4]

But limiting our food sources to that four-hundred-mile radius will lead to smaller menus and higher prices. The ideal—or optimal—geographic sources for our food are dictated by climate, cost of land and labor, abundance of resources, and nearby transportation networks.

Where our food comes from is also in relation to the size of our city. New York City can keep a multitude of producers relatively nearby because of the size of the market. New York's population of almost 9 million hungry inhabitants can support more producers than Abilene, Texas, with its population of almost 125,000, even though it's surrounded by a spacious landscape.

All of these factors, considered together, lower the cost and impact of food production, especially when you add scale to the mix. You can grow more per acre if the land and place provide ideal growing conditions. This is why you find oranges in Italy and in Southern California. Certain geographical areas become sites of specialization, combining suitable growing conditions with knowledge, practices, and relationships that yield higher-quality raw ingredients at lower costs. And, though not always the case, global distribution is often more sustainable and cost effective than forcing growth in unnatural environments. For example, bananas once grew in Iceland, but the cost of creating favorable growing conditions without significant financial incentives made local banana production unsustainable.

Of course, global food can become local if the conditions are right. Sometimes it's the movement of people that locates certain foods in a geographical area. Italian immigrants to the United States in the late nineteenth century brought Italian cuisine and a tomato supply chain to the Italian neighborhoods. A report published 2016 by the Royal Society indicated that almost 70 percent of the world's crops started out in locations other than where they are grown today. For example, tomatoes grown in Italy started out in South America, and the origin of potatoes (the scourge of Ireland) is Peru.[5] The report explains how countries that remained isolated maintained their own diverse native food lines, while those that were visited during the Age of Exploration experienced the greatest influx of crops, both as recipients of foreign crops and as exporters of native crops to the countries that sent the explorers. People bring food with them wherever they roam.

The Cost of Moving Food

The cost associated with moving food across long distances is usually the first calculation when determining the merits of local food production. Remember those local farmers' trucks that were travelling, half empty, to restaurants? If we consider cost per calorie again, driving that same truck in from a farm farther away, but filling it to the brim with orders from a dozen restaurants at once, is often a more budget-friendly solution. Empty space anywhere in the food supply chain isn't a good thing, whether in warehouses, on store shelves, or inside a tractor trailer.

The costs associated with transport make up about 10 percent of the total cost of a product, and they're driven by many variables—not only fuel.[6] Transport costs in winter are different than in summer because of the requirements to maintain controlled temperatures throughout the supply chain. And if transport costs go up by 10 percent, the cost of the product goes up about 20 percent. Besides the supply of a food commodity, fuel, and labor costs, the supply of ships plays a role in determining the cost to move that commodity. More grain, but not enough ships to move it, results in higher charter bids for those ships that still sail.

One study about transport and local food argues that a consumer who drives to a grocery store several miles away to buy vegetables will produce more carbon emissions than all the activities related to shipping the same vegetables from a much longer distance through a complex supply chain.[7] Other studies argue the contrary—the longer the supply chain, the greater the carbon emissions. But carbon footprints aren't the only impact distance has on the sustainability of our food supply chain. Fuel costs, transport modes, seasonality, and handling practices all weigh in for arguments on both sides.

Transport costs don't appear on our food labels yet. That's coming, but now our desire for knowledge about where our food comes from is evident in the food labeling debate. One example is the drive to state a product's origin on a food label. That's not a problem for most food producers, processors, and sellers, but what about meat that comes from animals raised in Colorado, fattened in Texas, and slaughtered in Kentucky? Or fish that is caught in New England and processed in Thailand? What part of that supply chain is local? And local to whom? How do customers think about the multiple circuits and stops that ingredients make on the way to our tables?

How do our emotions play out over such a complicated itinerary? Will a localized production system simplify things or make food more costly and limit the variety in our diets?

There are plenty of reasons to embrace global food rather than relying solely on local supply. Growing food not suited to our local environments may be more expensive and less efficient—not to mention less healthy and delicious. Coffee bushes produce small, less flavorful cherries outside of their natural environment, and they cost more to produce because of higher infrastructural and labor costs. What's more, a year of eating locally may lead to nutritional deficits if we live in a climate bereft of bananas. Those who don't see locally grown food as a necessary ingredient for a sustainable food system believe we should rejoice and benefit from a diverse food supply.

But making a calculated comparison of transportation costs for both local and global food is challenging: fuel costs vary, and it's almost impossible to determine whether trucks and containers are carrying full loads. Comparisons would need full assessments of environmental costs and a way of measuring the differences between the crops and proteins transported. The USDA has data for energy used for agricultural production, but even that data is conflated with measurements for direct and indirect energy usage. The USDA data states that agricultural producers consume 2 percent of the energy resources in the United States, and they use most of that energy to power equipment and machinery. According to the Giannini Foundation of Agricultural Economics at the University of California, a local system to provide the same per capita amount of corn to its residents would have to use 26 percent more land, 23 percent more fuel, and 29 percent more total inputs than the global system currently in place.[8]

Our instinct may be to look for local solutions, if for no other reason than to support our local economy.[9] But as soon as you convert non-crop land to food production, you impact local biodiversity. Another study by the Leopold Center argues that local and nonlocal food is price competitive for in-season food. During strawberry season, local berries often compete with nonlocal berries in price and quality.[10] And to add even more complexity to the local versus global debate, at least one academic, James McWilliams, a historian from Texas State University, points out the need to consider Life Cycle Assessment (LCA), the total carbon footprint of food production, to make sense of the pros and cons of local food.

How can we think about this whole local and global framework in the future? And how can we anticipate the location of our food supply with smart food logistics? It could be that pure distance will no longer weigh in as the leading consideration for evaluating what constitutes "good" or sustainable food. On one level, distance will become more abstract. Unable to juggle all the calculations for sending an item through a supply chain, we will opt for a simple way to view distance. Both perceived and actual distances will shorten. Our anxieties about the quality and character of our food system may be lessened by a new, technology-enabled sense of trust and transparency.

The desire for control over our lives makes us want more information about our food and those who produce it. Isn't that why we place so much stock in trust and transparency? Isn't this just what we're seeing in every other aspect of our culture, from ride sharing to finance to politics . . . to logistics?

One way to seek control over our food is to grow it ourselves. Three decades ago, my family ran a farm in Maine. With a short growing season and a languishing agricultural ecosystem, sustainability in that climate was elusive. But like most all farmers then, we were resourceful. We raised heritage sheep and pigs, toting clipboards along the icy pasture perimeter while we posted colored smudges on the fleecy backs of our flock of Cotswold sheep and affixed numbered tags to their ears. This was a routine practice (still used by many farmers today) that enabled us to keep track of which sheep were bred and when. Capturing this flock intelligence enabled us to plan our lambing season and predict the genetics and yield of that year's lamb crop.

Those clipboards found their way into metal filing cabinets after we hand-entered the numbers into our desktop computer. Aside from planning that year's lambing season, there wasn't much else we could do with our data. But there would be now; farmers are capturing much more data, using it smartly, and finding that there may be a future in farming after all.

Technology has shaped how we grow and produce our food ever since the first fire warmed a haunch of bison. But the speed of technological evolution went into high gear when a convergence of technologies enabled changes in transport, preservation, safety, and agricultural productivity. These moments in technological evolution created "revolutions" in the food supply system, moments when agricultural productivity sharply increased and food became safe to eat and able to reach consumers within days, not months, of harvest.

The world is pretty good at increasing food productivity. We now produce more per acre than ever before due to technological innovations. According to the USDA, global agricultural productivity continues to increase, although slower on average than during the initial decades of the industrialization of agriculture. So while we feel certain that these technological evolutions will continue, we are less certain of what it means to live in a digital world. Nowadays, a relatively small number of farms grow most of the food we eat, and this trend comes with both good news and bad news. Having been successful at increasing yields ever since the eighteenth century, farmers have demonstrated that they know how to get more from their land than ever before. For example, although the number of dairy cows has steadily declined since 2010, dairies have found ways to produce more milk per cow.[11]

The bad news is, some economists argue, that productivity gains from the technology that has existed since the Industrial Revolution are at their end. As with all mature technologies, many agricultural technologies are winding down their impact on output from soil-based agriculture which is a bit worrisome for those of us who see the need to feed a growing world population with its variable and often capricious diets. To achieve the productivity increases needed to feed all of us in 2050, it seems we need another technological revolution, similar to the industrial one, to ignite significant productivity increases. Thus, the digital revolution, agtech, and foodtech. The new optimizers: Big Data and connectivity.

The New Production Optimizers: Agtech

The convergence of Big Data and connectivity is uprooting our traditional outlook on food production and the places where it occurs. Instead of Central California or China as the source of our lettuce, we now consider other locations closer to our tables. Aware of the limitations and stresses on our current food systems, individuals, companies, and governments have been rallying resources to address the limitations of growing food using traditional practices in traditional locations. Technology will continue to increase productivity, and it is now beginning to help us address environmental sustainability as well.

Agricultural technology, "agtech," addresses the known inefficiencies and unprofitability of farms, and in some cases it has allowed us to reconsider where farming takes place. In 2017, investors poured more than $1.5 billion into technology-infused solutions for agriculture.[12] The number of deals for everything from soil sensors to driverless tractors is impressive, but it will take a while to see the results of these ventures, as smart irrigation and new seed germination technology are somewhat confined within growing seasons. Investors hope technology will increase farm productivity, sustainability, and nutrition with the assistance of Big Data, the Internet of Things (IoT), and the ability to track and trace raw materials throughout the system.

When food companies acquired digital tools in the 1950s, they waded into processing in much the same way society waded into general computing. Before chips got cheaper and network speeds got faster, most farmers were unable to afford the software and hardware to make their farms work smarter. Even during the 1990s, when my family ran a farm in Maine, only large farms with revenues over $500,000 could afford computer systems to optimize their operations and gather useful data. Now, with ubiquitous personal computing, food producers have a chance to utilize data to increase productivity and profitability—and even fabricate new foods.

On the ground, precision agriculture, the use of digital technology to improve agriculture, is making traditional farming more productive. It's "precise" because it considers variable soils, crop characteristics, and irrigation requirements. All of these factors and more create the opportunity to maximize productivity through technology while utilizing sustainable practices.

Drones, for example, are becoming useful tools for farmers who want to improve the visibility of their crops. AgEagle makes a drone that can survey a farmer's fields to provide images that improve field management and crop health. Some companies make tools that enable farmers to integrate weather data with irrigation systems and other farm machinery so inputs and practices can be implemented according to precise requirements. Farm equipment manufacturers are making "smart" machines that capture data and use it in ways that enable tractors and harvesters to process more calories with less energy. Drones, smart machines, and robots are all coming to agriculture to make raw ingredient production more sustainable and productive. Blue River's Lettucebot thins lettuce using precise applications of chemicals. Using water and artificial intelligence, Taylor

Farms in California has robots harvesting heads of lettuce. This means the food supply chain—or part of it, at least—will operate from the same production sites but with greater predictability and, potentially, less waste and labor.

Imagine a meter of soil with its own pesticide and irrigation. The mass treatment of land leading to runoff and waste could be eliminated. Farmers are now collecting on-farm data that will enable practical and useful agtech solutions like this one. Big Data on weather history, soil conditions, and plant nutrient requirements now make it easy for a farmer to increase productivity while saving on labor and material costs. With the surge in data-gathering sensors and smart vehicles, agriculture on the ground might be able to survive the coming demographic changes that will shape increased demand. With the new digital tools, farmers have the opportunity to become more productive and profitable outside the traditional farming model, as an engineer or producer developing a new operating system.

The Data Dilemma

Agricultural data, though, is fraught with inconsistencies and incompatibilities. There is no data standard for several reasons. Equipment manufacturers regard their data-gathering methodology as proprietary, and as we'll see later in the book, the traditional food-manufacturing culture reinforces the notion that supply and supply chains shouldn't be transparent since transparency may expose competitive advantages. There is a movement within the industry that supports open systems, but those who support the proprietary model argue that data is valuable and needs to be regarded as a fungible asset. In other words, if farmers fail to keep their data proprietary, they may lose the potential to leverage its value in the market.

Agricultural equipment manufacturers and related companies already offer data collection for selected activities on the farm. John Deere's tractor technology enables farmers to use GPS and weather data to precisely target areas of the field for specific, relevant treatment. But that data doesn't neatly merge with the data collected by other devices, and it won't capture crops that aren't harvested by a sophisticated tractor. There are plenty of advantages to selling data or making it available, at the farmer's discretion, to third parties. For example, an insurance company may use data to offer reduced premiums to farmers avoiding certain risky practices.

Farmobile is one agricultural data company that operates within the proprietary model. As a startup working closely with farmers and equipment manufacturers, Farmobile intends to connect the data-gathering sensors on a farm so both the farmer and the equipment manufacturers can improve performance of the machines and the humans that operate them. Matt Kamphoefner, the VP of sales and business development at Farmobile, sees on-the-ground data gathering as a way to enable farmers to become smarter, owning their own data for improved performance. Kamphoefner intends to develop a data standard for the information a farmer collects on his or her farm. He refers to "automatic electronic field records" (AEFR) that a mobile device will capture in real time and integrate into a portable database that the farmer could monetize. Kamphoefner envisions a time when a farmer can download, for a fee, a "playlist" of agriculture data as a way to see how a crop performs on a specific farm.

But Farmobile's position on proprietary data contrasts with MIT CityFarm's efforts to create an open data systems platform for farmers. Caleb Harper, director of the Open Agriculture Initiative, believes transformative improvements in food production can be achieved by applying data and technology. MIT's OpenAg engineers, software developers, and data scientists have job titles that mirror the digital world, not the world of soil scientists and agronomists: Farmer of Electrons, Farmer of Boxes, and Farmer of Software, to name a few. Harper's title is, predictably, Farmer of Farmers. The project's enclosed tabletop growing systems become "food computers," and larger versions, the size of shipping containers, become "food servers." The warehouse-sized versions become "food datacenters." The project has spawned a language for food production that may reflect the emergence of a new agriculture that brings together an interdisciplinary group of experts from both the digital and nondigital agricultural communities. The Open Ag group offers imaginative ways of talking about this mash-up, such as "on-demand, fingerprinted food." Or "digital farms" and an "Open Phenome Library."[13]

MIT's history as a land grant university has been defined by its reputation as a leader in science and technology. But not until the surge of consumer interest in all topics related to food did MIT discover the opportunity to leverage its knowledge of the digital world to solve problems in the analog world of plants and animals. Returning to its roots, you could say. Now they host conferences with the Culinary Institute of America and engage

with chefs and farmers to explore how to become part of the food movement. Of course, MIT isn't the only academic institution hard at work in
the field of agtech and food tech. UC Davis, Cornell, and Texas A&M are all
developing programs and producing research on the topic of digital farms.

At MIT, Harper's project would like to increase the number of farmers by
providing data to improve outcomes for agriculture. He uses closed aquaponic and aeroponic growing systems, sensors, and software to control,
measure, and digitize the process of growing plants. The data gathered in
these growing systems would be shared, for free, on platforms that farmers
or anyone interested in farming could access. Calling the process "food
computing," Harper refers to the data for specific growing conditions as
"recipes" that other farmers could use to install in their growing systems,
whether vertical or horizontal. Traditional farmers may find Harper's ideas
too abstract for and antithetical to the belief that farming is as much an art
as it is a science.

Not everyone in the traditional agriculture community is wild about
MIT's approach to reinventing the food system. It's way too soon to know
how the competing platforms of open and closed data systems will form
the future of food production. But it is clear that farming is on the cusp of
yet another revolution.

And as we enter that revolution, we're upending not only agriculture
and industrialized food, but also our common conceptions of where food
comes from. Traditionally, we got food from the sea, from the ground, and
from beasts that foraged on the ground. We still do, but now food producers are also appearing on floating farms, on city rooftops, inside shipping
containers, and on our kitchen counters. What's happening here? For one
thing, land costs determine where food grows, and an acre in New York
City can cost one hundred times more than an acre in Iowa.[14] Land is so
costly in cities that prices are expressed in dollars per square foot, not per
acre. In 2000, farmland in Iowa sold for $1,857 per acre.[15] In the same year,
land in Columbus Circle, at the center of New York City, sold for approximately $2,300 per *square foot* (nearly $100 million per acre).[16] The idea of
growing carrots on land that costly would be prohibitive if land costs were
the only factor. But they aren't. People want to see their food growing, and
the idea of using urban spaces in new ways—like all those ugly, flat rooftops in cities—is appealing. Not to mention that transporting carrots from
Iowa or central California must add up.

Growing Food Everywhere

So today, not all farmers work the soil to produce food. Vertical and enclosed urban farms are sprouting up all across the world. One of the companies building these growing platforms, Controlled-Environments Agriculture (CEA), as the new soil acres are called, is Gotham Greens.[17] It has built growing systems in Brooklyn, Queens, and Chicago. Founded in 2009, Gotham Greens operates on the assumption that food production need not occur on traditional dirt farms. Its large, commercial-scale greenhouses sit atop buildings in urban landscapes and grow leafy greens using LED lights powered by solar panels. Because they are enclosed, these urban farms are protected from pests and other environmental conditions that open-air farmers contend with every day. And Gotham Greens and other such companies want to go big. These farms produce hundreds of thousands of pounds of leafy greens, berries, and herbs for urban customers, some of which are grocery stores like Whole Foods and even, surprisingly, Walmart.

Growing plants in greenhouses isn't all that innovative, but locating the greenhouses on rooftops in dense urban areas to shorten the "Last Mile" delivery might be an improvement. These new ventures illustrate how where we produce our food directly impacts the supply chain and food logistics. The idea certainly appeals to advocates of local food production, and any efforts to improve food production are laudable. And the use of these farms to produce leafy greens and other foods that suffer in transport makes sense in terms of high-value products that will forego their large carbon footprint on the way to market. One logical use case for these farms are those regions in cold-climate zones, such as in Norway where vertical farms produce strawberries. In the Netherlands, vertical farms can overcome the lack of arable land for crop production.

One wonders, though, if Gotham Greens' urban rooftop gardens depend too heavily on urban rooftops—after all, there are only so many rooftops to take over, even in New York. And the flipside of closed growing systems is the risk of contamination or invasive insects that would have a field day in one of those self-contained greenhouses. And while it would undoubtedly be a problem on a private balcony garden, in a commercial outfit like Gotham Greens, contamination would spell disaster. The risks of monocultures are not specific to corn crops in the Midwest or in China.

A contained growing environment is also the platform for Freight Farms, a venture started in 2009 by Jon Friedman and Brad McNamara that combines some of Harper's ideas with the idea of growing food in shipping containers. Not stuck on a rooftop, shipping containers are mobile and scalable, as long as there's room to spread them out or stack them up. In growing containers spread throughout the United States, Freight Farms uses hydroponic systems (water instead of soil) and LED lights to grow plants. Its sensors collect growing data that farmers can view through the Farmhand mobile app.[18]

AeroFarms, an urban farming company founded in 2015, uses aeroponics, as one might expect from its name.[19] Aeroponics joins a list of growing technologies that don't rely on soil on the ground: hydroponics, aquaponics, and aeroponics. "Ponics," from Latin, means "work." Instead of working the soil to grow plants, these modern farmers work water and air. Hydroponics grows plants in water using root systems to pull nutrients into the plant. Aquaponics also uses water, but it adds nutrient fertilizer from fish raised in the water. Aeroponics uses water not by immersing the root systems in water but by suspending the root systems in a humid environment where water sprays fill the air with moisture. All three of these systems are used for greenhouses and vertical farms in cities.

Located in New Jersey, the state still called the Garden State, Aerofarms produces indoor, enclosed farms that can be built inside homes, offices, warehouses, or just about anywhere else. Its growing units can be stacked or spread out, and the company is keen to use industrial spaces such as old nightclubs or paintball factories. Schools can buy their systems as educational platforms and perhaps even for food production.

At SXSW in 2017, a Los Angeles startup brought its farm to Austin. Called Local Roots, the company promises to produce food year-round, "undoing the commodification of the food industry" and "eliminating supply chain risks" by building a network of farms.[20] Using its "Terrafarm" solution, Local Roots sells its produce through restaurants in Southern California. SpaceX uses a Terrafarm to produce its greens. These innovative gardens may seem like an ideal solution, but they're still fighting back some nasty weeds. Over the past few years, early leaders in the field, including PodPonics in Atlanta, FarmedHere in Chicago, and Local Garden in Vancouver have shut down. Some had design issues, while others started too early, when hardware costs were much higher. Gotham Greens and AeroFarms look promising, but they haven't raised comparable cash hoards or outlined similarly ambitious plans yet. By the time you read this, they may be installing acres of growing platforms in your city. Vertical, container, and other enclosed and moveable farms are appearing faster than we imagined, even though few are close to profitable and crop diversity is limited.

Once considered a novel and small-scale option for food production, these new urban farms are quickly gathering momentum. Initiatives launched in San Francisco and cities around the world are making plans for ways to integrate food production into their master plans. In the Netherlands, an urban farm project called Fresh Care Convenience was announced in 2017 between Phillips Lighting and a large fresh food company, Staay Food Group—the construction of Europe's first large-scale vertical farm.[21] Several grocery stores in Germany are adding indoor farms designed by Infarm, a startup located in Berlin. And in Texas, two indoor farm companies are setting up farms, one in Abeline and another in Lockhart. These two ventures illustrate how these projects benefit from private/public partnerships. Both cities view the farm projects as sources of economic development and provide incentives in the form of subsidies and land. The Brightfarms project in Abilene will be the first hydroponic farm in Texas, a state known for its droughts. These ventures also enable food production in unexpected places: a shrimp farm in Nebraska, Rock Creek Aquaculture, shortens the supply chains for seafood from oceans far away and provides some local jobs. And Plenty, headquartered in South San Francisco, combines LED lighting, hydroponics, tech funders, and vertical farming to explore how to scale these ventures so that they are both environmentally and economically sustainable.

For now, these ventures are sticking to the leafy greens and herbs that are well suited to these platforms. But what happens when the market is saturated with culinary lettuce, but customers need squash, potatoes, and radishes? And will all these contained, vertical, urban farms be able to scale? Will they produce food at prices competitive with supermarkets like Costco and Walmart, which are both major players in organic food markets? Looks more like a reality than ever before, though if any of these ventures that depend upon scaling to be financially sustainable succeed, they will need to consider what to do with a surplus of food. Will they require transport of produce *out* of the city once they've brought seeds and inputs *into* the city for the purpose of growing food? Chances are these friction points will be addressed as engineers and consumers discover whom they want as food producers and where and how they will shop for food. And none of these ventures has yet to fully calculate an ROI for the long term.

Even traditional greenhouses may indeed fill a much-needed gap in the supply chain sourcing world, especially during times of climate change. They aren't new, but they are now full of sensors and LED lighting systems. Growing food in resource-deficient environments might be the biggest opportunity for the supply chain. All of these ventures promote the idea of farming with less water, no pesticides, increased productivity over land-based farming, and tighter control over the growing process and environment.

Handheld Farming

Many of these new "farms" integrate mobile devices for produce monitoring. Say you have a microfarm in your apartment connected to sensors that send growing conditions. You might learn your lettuce needs water, so you send instructions to your microfarm to adjust the micro-irrigation system to the proper levels for that type of plant. Or you're a commercial farmer, and your smartphone tells you that there is too much moisture in the field at the far end of your farm; you decide not to irrigate that day. Is this handheld farming the future? Will growers miss the grounding experience of sensing moisture with their own hands? New farmers don't think so.

The future of such systems could get complicated once you consider what success might look like for these ventures. Imagine that Freight Farms' containers become backyard food production houses scaled for personal food, with enough produce year-round to feed a family or city block. Would that eliminate the trips to the grocery store? Solve for food deserts? Or will the novelty of these solutions dissipate, leaving behind only the routine of tending to one's own garden?

Not only are we growing food in new places, such as shipping containers, but we are also intrigued by—though not yet sold on—the idea of producing our own food at home. Even in our own kitchens. A number of startups, such as SproutsIO, are offering personal growing systems that fit in a condo or home kitchen with the ingredients for growing herbs, greens, and even tomatoes. Using technology similar to that of vertical farms, these new systems offer apps so you can monitor the moisture content of the soil in your kitchen garden. SproutsIO even allows personal taste profiles to customize the SproutsIO growing system. In the long term, moisture, produce, and personal taste profiles may be monitored by Alexa or a smart home monitoring system similar to Nest. Let's not consider what might happen in a power outage. And what about when we go on vacation? Will our pet sitters be willing to keep our lettuce alive, too? As the novelty wears thin, we may opt for convenience and keep having others grow our food for us.

The New Farmers

We're not all born farmers, or at least not since we began to move to cities. But farmers are about to change, not only in the skills they possess but also in the tools and platforms they use to produce raw materials for the supply chain. Most of the teams that work in these new farms don't come from traditional agriculture. They are young and rarely have degrees in agronomy from land-grant universities. Instead, they have a background in digital technology and come to the world of agriculture with some fresh ideas.

Farming may just be the next cool occupation, combining maker culture, social enterprise, and the desire to get one's hands dirty. From protein to plant life to fish, these innovations in food production will change the food supply chain in many ways. Urban farms—whether aquaponic or aeroponic, in shipping containers under bridges, or on rooftop greenhouses—will almost eliminate the Last Mile. But in turn, storage facilities, processing companies, and transportation infrastructure will need to adapt to these new production sites, and the next generation of farmers may just be the team to make it happen.

These new farmers won't look like any we have known in the past. They will be younger and more diverse. They will grow food wherever they can find room, and they will use technology and data in ways never imagined before. Jennifer Farah, founder of SproutsIO, is developing a personal farm, an indoor garden system that personalizes produce with flavor profiles that you manage from your mobile device. Automatic seed refilling and Wi-Fi connectivity allow these farms and the new farmers to operate outside traditional agriculture.

These new farmers will be receptive to transparency and motivated to adopt new, digital tools. They may make more money selling data from their operations than from food, which they will produce in higher quantities with less land and labor and fewer inputs. Some will have engineering degrees with experience in business and science sprinkled throughout their LinkedIn profiles. And some will grow food in farms that would have been unimaginable a decade ago.

Caleb Harper at MIT, Jennifer Farah of SproutsIO, and Eric Ellestad of Local Roots Farms may be our new farmers. Eric, like other modern farmers, has a degree in the sciences and business. Jennifer has a degree in architecture. These are entrepreneurs who are coming to food production as engineers, scientists, artists, and savvy businesspeople. They are risk takers, a different sort of breed than the traditional farmers who have learned to play it safe. It may take generations to restructure the economics of farming, but the fourth revolution of agriculture may provide the needed tools, optimized by those accelerators—Big Data and connectivity.

Changes in the way we produce food are occurring on the ground, and they're not necessarily driven by governments, policies, or traditional food institutions like agricultural organizations and universities. Some innovations are coming from engineers and biologists who promise to solve the problems related to animal slaughter, energy, and the environment. Some of the new initiatives come from nonprofits or private investor groups that are not mired in government bureaucracies or traditional ways of thinking about food. Farmer-entrepreneur-scientists have found they can eliminate the traditional farm platform altogether through lab-grown steaks, replacing ranchers' corrals with petri dishes.[22]

Are there consequences of this shift? Sure. The old institutions that hold our knowledge of agricultural science may soon be untapped or ignored, causing these new entrepreneurs to make avoidable mistakes. If it becomes too attractive and lucrative to run a digitally based urban farm, will we lose even more land-based farmers and thus lose some diversity in our agricultural industry? How do we keep both soil and soil-free growing systems in an ecosystem that provides a resilient food system? How will we feel when the sleek features of a robot replace our image of a farmer? And what will happen to those traditional farmers standing in their fields? Will some adapt these new digital tools and learn to use data from scanners and sensors? Already in debt as a result of buying outdated farm equipment and awaiting payouts from crop insurance, will those farmers be able to invest in the new technologies? We might consider a transition plan, one that brings along the deep knowledge of traditional farming while training and financing those farmers who want to migrate their farms into the digital age.

From Lab or Fab to Plate

It's not just the soil-grown, farmer-nurtured food that's undergoing a revolution. Memphis Meats and New Harvest are two young companies that grow meat in laboratories. Actually, they culture it from animal cells to grow "real" meat. Uma Valeti, the CEO of Memphis Meats (located in the San Francisco Bay area, not Memphis, Tennessee) is a cardiologist who leads a team of scientists developing what they call "clean" meat—meat they allege is more sustainable and free of harmful ingredients while addressing concerns about animal welfare in our food system.[23] Isha Datar, a cellular biologist, founded New Harvest, another startup that wants to produce meat, milk, eggs, and other animal products. Both companies run nonprofits so they can receive donations during these early stages of research and testing.

These first efforts to bypass traditional farm models are expensive: Memphis Meats' first burgers cost $325,000 to produce.[24] In 2017, the company rolled out its first lab-grown poultry, with one pound of lab-grown chicken costing $9,000.[25] The theory is that these costs will come down as those products are produced at scale, but it's unclear when that will occur. As this book goes to press, prices for lab-grown meat and plant-based meat are steadily going down and these products are becoming available through fast food chains and grocery stores.

Mosa Meats, located in the Netherlands, is a collaboration with scientists at Maastricht University. Their team hopes to have an affordable burger grown from bovine cells within the next five years. Without the need for animals as a source for meat, these companies argue they can scale up production fairly efficiently. They don't need more animals, just a few more cells. These new ventures are working on finding the sweet spot between cost and taste, which isn't easy since you can buy hamburger meat at your grocery store for about $2.50 per pound.

But cellular agriculture is just one of the ways food production is changing hands. As an alternative to growing meat from animal cells, other scientists are creating meat-like proteins from plants. The possibilities seem endless, but two startups, Impossible Foods and Beyond Meat, have taken the plant idea to our plates, as they did for our Texas dinner.[26] Available in some supermarkets, these plant burgers differ from the meat-free staple, the veggie burger. The biochemists that engineered the new meat have been able to create the visual, textural, and sensorial characteristics of real meat. As long as you don't have your heart set on a marbled T-bone steak, the plant-based meat burger is pretty good and an improvement over years of veggie burgers. And if plant burgers seem too old school, you can find your protein in bugs. Insect protein is on the rise as the new industry seeks a way to scale production.[27] Called microlivestock, insects as a substitute for animal protein still meet resistance in certain cultures. If large-scale insect production and processing improves and innovates ways to integrate the protein into our diets so that the bugginess of the food product is subtle, then perhaps, maybe, we'll accept Impossible Bugs in the same way as we now accept Impossible Burgers. If bugs are too down to earth for our tastes, algae grown in space will develop a new vertical supply chain. As with fish farms, these new protein producers will shake up the supply chain, begging the question about the future of fields for grazing and feed-lots for fattening.

Hand-in-hand with lab-grown protein come questions about another controversial lab-based food activity: genetic modification. Technology, mostly digital and biochemical, is providing new tools for improving our food production systems. While farmers have been successful at increasing productivity, these new tools enable farmers, or food engineers as they may soon be called, to control the quality of our food. Until now, genetic modification has been a farmer's method of selecting stock that improves the overall herd. A farmer selects breeding stock on the basis of rate of weight gain, vigor, and carcass quality. But these improvements occur over successive breeding cycles that take years to fully realize.

Engineered Food 2.0

New companies such as Ginko Bioworks work in the biotech industry to genetically modify organisms shamelessly and with impunity. While Monsanto struggles to redeem itself from decades of bad PR, lawsuits, and regulatory imbroglio, these new companies seek ways to genetically modify our food with the intention of improving the environment, enhancing food safety, or increasing agricultural productivity. These social values make

GMO food digestible by many who previously viewed the practice as harmful to society, not to mention animals and humans alike.

The arguments both for and against genetic modification of food have complicated the adoption of the technology and obscured the science that supports the process. While we continue to debate GMO foods, a newer technology called CRISPR (Clustered Regularly Interspaced Short Palindromic Repeats) has gained attention for its ability to create similar improvements without introducing genes from other organisms, as in genetic modification. CRISPR essentially allows a scientist to edit an RNA gene sequence, which is different from GMOs. The potential for CRISPR is not yet fully explored, but many producers feel it may very well transform food production. Genetically designed food, edited through CRISPR, could enable oranges to grow in Alaska, wheat to become pest resistant, eggs to contain more nutrients, and bread products to be completely gluten free. All this change at the production level is bound to shake up the supply chain, shift production locations, and make seasonal foods an outmoded concept.[28]

Genetic editing of seeds may lead to food with higher nutritional value at lower unit sizes. And in the livestock world, breeders are now working on smaller livestock with more nutritional value. Three companies are working on small chickens because large carcass sizes cause chickens to outweigh their performance as animals. A condition of oversized poultry called woody breast has caused the poultry industry to reconsider the strategy of selecting broiler stock for growth rates and breast size.[29] Making food grow too fast causes the protein to become rubbery; smaller chickens just taste better than the big, fast-growing variety. Since they produce less meat per chicken, though, it's likely that the small chicken will cost more, putting those tasty nuggets out of reach of many customers.

Aviagen has copyrighted poultry types with brand names such as Yield Plus and a catalogue called the Specialty Male Portfolio.[30] In addition to Yield Plus, Aviagen is producing a slower-growing brand to respond to the demand for small chickens. In January 2017, the company announced its appointment of a manager of the "slow-growing poultry market segment." Other breeders, such as Hubbard Breeders and Cobb-Vantress, are working on these new, slow broilers. The poultry supply chain will need another year to accommodate to this longer production cycle.

All these efforts to change where, how, and who produces our food have an effect on our food supply chain. When Tyson moves to produce lab meat instead of chickens, our protein supply chain will lurch in a new direction along with the humans who currently work in its livestock facilities. And the growing acceptance of tech in food production, including GMOs and CRISPR, makes this transition possible now more than at any time in past.

While these innovations may dramatically increase our ability to produce large quantities of food at the standards consumers demand, the implications for the food supply chain are hardly clear at this point. How will our plant protein world find enough space to grow all the plant material needed to make enough protein for our growing population? And what happens when our palates become accustomed to these lab meats and the need for livestock dissipates altogether? Land use will most likely undergo a significant reallocation from grazing space to something else. National parks? Housing? And will the only place schoolchildren see a Longhorn heifer be our local zoo? These new ventures, if successful, will probably move on from beef to other proteins such as chicken and pork. The impact of lab meat production upon agricultural biodiversity is as yet unclear and unexplored. But one thing is for certain: supply chain designers and logistics managers will have to restructure the flow of protein to our plates.

Food Deserts to Food Oases?

Another, more welcome consequence of the arrival of digital food production may be the disappearance of food deserts. Space, distance, and proximity all play into the idea of food deserts. The term emerged as a way to describe a lack of access to healthy, nutritious food, usually in poor and minority neighborhoods. You may live in a neighborhood with a grocery store that lacks fresh produce; that's a desert maker. The USDA defines a food desert as an area where at least 33 percent of the population lacks either a vehicle or a grocery store within a mile of their home and/or a car. In some situations, like in mid-Texas, the distance may be longer.[31]

The first mention of the concept of a food desert appeared during the 1990s as urban planners and urban policy makers began to notice the lack of access to food for certain demographics.[32] The Food Poverty Eradication Bill, the Farm Bill, and the Healthy Food Financing Initiative are all examples of government efforts to address food deserts during the past two decades. International, federal, state, and local studies exploring food access have gained visibility and raised public awareness. This is certainly a supply chain issue, if you consider that food isn't being supplied to the areas in question.

But the desert has complications. The reason deserts aren't easily filled with healthy food sometimes has more to do with transportation, pricing, lifestyle, trust, and community relationships than with mere proximity. In more than a few cases, healthy food stores are built in deserts only to find that they lose money and customers. Federal programs such as the Special Supplemental Nutrition Program (SNAP) and Special Supplemental Nutrition Program for Women, Infants, and Children (WIC) attempt to solve for the economic reasons that healthy food isn't accessible in some areas.[33] In early 2018, the United States was considering a change in its SNAP program so that low income families would receive boxes of food instead of money. Who knows, maybe we're about to see a new curated food box join the many other food boxes on the way to our doors.

New research is emerging that offers more holistic assessments of food deserts and incorporates a range of solutions to improve access. One of these studies uses mapping software as a tool to represent the geography of food deserts alongside resident behavior, regional mobility, and demography. The most impactful solution presented in the report was the addition of a grocery store in combination with the willingness of a resident to walk at least a mile, or 1600 meters.[34]

One solution is to mobilize grocery stores, put them on wheels or rails, and move them right into the deserts. One startup in our Challenge Prize competition, Grit Grocery, does just that. A new take on Meals on Wheels, these mobile grocery stores could even target the mobile inventory for specific ethnic cuisines. A sort of personal grocery store, this solution is not so much about where food is produced, but about the distribution of food (more about that in chapter 5). Some efforts to bring food production into communities are a result of the desire to bring urban populations closer to their food as part of a larger educational and social mission. In the same spirit of traditional community gardens, these social projects are likely to remain as we seek a refuge from our digital food and yearn for the human side of our food.

Technology—knowledge about science and how to apply it to food production—has always been present in our food system. But the speed of innovation has increased, creating anxiety for some of us who worry that we are unaware of the consequences of the technology we allow into our lives. The replacement of humans, both physically and mentally, by hardware and software is also worrisome to those of us who wonder what will be left for us to do in the future. Surely we will have new jobs and a higher purpose to fulfill in the world. Or perhaps not.

Farmers today can produce enough food to feed the world now and in the foreseeable future. As the United Nations' Food and Agriculture Organization (FAO) testifies, we can grow enough food by investing in technology, putting more arable land into production, and increasing the intensity of agriculture.[35] Then, central to the premise of this book, we'll be able to distribute all the food we produce to all those that need food.

Farming in the Digital Age

Farmers on larger farms are being held accountable for damage to the environment and the harmful effects of industrially grown food. The idea of growing food with practices associated with factories evolved from being the *sine qua non* of traditional farming to the *bête noire* of modern farming. As our cultural values changed from admiration of technological progress to longing for romanticized rural practices, we began to use the adjective "industrial" to imply lower quality food. If consumers had their way, today's farms would maintain their technology-supported levels of productivity while returning to traditional, rural practices and delivering only natural, "unprocessed" food. This is enough to challenge the emerging generation of young farmers, and they have three principal issues to address as they look for solutions.

The first is the consolidation of food production. Most of the farms today are small. About 90 percent of all American farmers run small family farms and earn less than $350,000 in gross cash farm income (GCFI).[36] What's more, the FAO estimated in 2014 that 1 percent of all the farms in the world control over 65 percent of the land used for food production.[37] This amalgamation of companies that make and supply our food is continuing, contributing to dependence upon a few farms for most of our protein and to control of food production by global companies. Some of this aggregation is a result of poor economic conditions that push publicly held companies to look for ways to increase stock values. Combining forces is becoming a strategy for improving profits.

The second issue is consumer demand. As demand and behavior change (recently, people falling out of love with kale and embracing meat broth), the supply chain has to find new supplies and producers and figure out how to get all the ingredients needed to reformulate or produce new food, all while providing the level of transparency that improves trust between those who produce and those who consume.

The third issue is the aging of American farmers. With the majority of the agriculture industry headed for retirement, who will grow our food in the future? How will they do it, and on what kind of farm? The number of farmers has been steadily decreasing since the early twentieth century, falling 4.3 percent in the United States between 2007 and 2013. And those who remain are not spring chickens. Between 1982 and 2012, the average age of American farmers rose from 50.5 to 58.3.[38] Today's farmers are old and ripe with wisdom and experience, but they're about to retire or sell. That makes the Caleb Harpers of the world anomalies, or harbingers, depending upon your expectations for the future of farming. If we accept engineers as the new farmers and scaling of digital, non-soil-based farming in cities as the new platform, we may soon see a new, digital, distributed, scaled food production system that will replace the industrial, environmentally damaging farm of the past century.

The Smart Food City

Cities are also working on ways to include food systems and distribution in their urban plans for the future. In 2015, the city of Atlanta, Georgia, hired its first Director of Urban Agriculture, signaling a commitment to food systems as part of their urban infrastructure and planning process, and more cities are coming to the table. Officers in the area of sustainability are thinking more about urban landscapes that incorporate plans for producing, storing, and distributing food within an overall vision for the future. Other cities are looking at how food fits into their model for a Smart City. In 2011, Chattanooga, Tennessee, announced a competition for ideas about reimagining its food system, and they produced an assessment of all resources that could be included in a new Smart City food system. More cities are waking up to the idea that more than smart traffic management systems are needed to create smart ways to move things in our future cities.

The Smart Cities movement began in the 1970s with the use of demographic and economic data to find ways to address poverty within the urban landscape. Now, with the growth of digital networks, the accumulation of digitized data, artificial intelligence, and mapping software, cities are assigning "smartness" to a new vision for connectivity. At first these developments included transportation and network access, but now the connection of sensors, point-of-sale capture, drones, and robots all point to the increased interest in thinking about the food supply chain as another utility that could make food distribution to cities a smart move. Typically, urban planners designed cities that offered functionality for human transport—mass transit, parking systems, community gardens, and green spaces—but didn't consider all these as part of an urban food system. Agritecture, founded by Henry Gordon-Smith, is a hip consulting company in Brooklyn, New York that develops food-smart cities.

As water and fuel have conduits into cities, why not food? Perhaps the smarter city will have all the inputs for an urban farm delivered underground with waste going directly to efficient bio-fueled generators. The really, really smart city will need planners across multiple disciplines, including nutrition, architecture, and computer science.

The dislocation of supply and demand will need a solution as we find ways to feed the growing global population. The practices of dragging the ocean floor and pumping inputs, fertilizers, and pesticides into our soil and hormones into our animals won't satisfy our hunger or our new sensitivities for sustainability. Short of growing food on Mars, we will be finding ways to leverage digital technology to grow better, cheaper food in places we live and work. In some cases, the Last Mile may be no miles.

3 Everything in the Middle

Argentina is the country we associate with meat and gauchos. Ever since the Spanish conquistadors brought their cattle to South America in the 1500s, Argentinians have been occupied with becoming one of the largest producers and consumers of red meat. Even now, a visitor to Buenos Aires finds a culture of BBQ, with haunches of beef and pork grilling and filling the air with the smoky aroma of meat ready to eat. Early in the morning, trucks move up and down quiet streets cleared from the previous night's revelry, filled with firewood to replenish the *parillas*. Meat is just about everyone's business. Just ask Ruben.

Ruben works at a pork processing plant housed in two buildings in Lomas del Mirador, a neighborhood of Buenos Aires, Argentina. His plant houses meat grinders, chopping tables, walk-in refrigerators, and sausage stuffing equipment. Trucks rumble in and out of the loading dock delivering Argentinian beef and pork as Ruben's team members, dressed in their white uniforms, trim, chop, and mince meat into the various products on order from customers in Buenos Aires. He is hard at work in the part of our food supply chain that makes most of us uncomfortable: processing, packaging, and storing food.

Ruben and his team take care of all the processing their sausages require for a consumer who's planning a barbecue, but if those sausages are going on a pizza or into a ready-to-heat jambalaya, then they're not done yet. Even when we consider that our food has to be processed at some point along the supply chain, we may not consider how many times it's processed. We think the familiar food brand is the processor, but that company may employ countless other secondary processors you've never heard of along the way. Called "food manufacturing" by some in the business, many food-processing companies operate quietly between ingredients and well-known food brands. Consider tomato sauce: the tomatoes are sorted, boxed, cooked, pureed, stored, combined with other ingredients such as cheese and spices, canned, boxed again, stored, and packaged again. That pizza in Joe's shop incorporates dozens of ingredients that have been transformed along the way to New York City.

Transformation

Some talk about this part of our food supply chain as one of intermediation, when the flow of our food encounters activities that intervene, interrupt, and handle our food on the way to our plates. During this phase, our food is handled, packed, processed, transformed, packaged, and stored. So many people, so many hands. So many opportunities for, well, anything.

The processing and manufacturing of food relieves us of our romantic, personal, and human connection with our dinner. We whinge at the image of a hamburger oozing with pink slime and cringe at extruders as they draw out strings of bread dough to make puffy buns. The idea of stainless steel paddles blending seaweed into ice cream to enhance its texture just doesn't seem logical, much less desirable. Today our minds and bodies tell us that we want minimally processed food, made close by, that is untampered and unfettered and unadulterated. God forbid our avocado meets a robot that almost surgically removes its large pit, or that the seed disappears altogether because of an overaccommodating genetic engineer. Oh, that did happen, when Marks and Spencer announced its pitless avocado in December 2017.

Food evangelists today preach the merits of minimal processing. Simplicity, they say, leaves food in its pristine, natural condition. One of these evangelists is food writer Michael Pollan. His first rule for healthy eating is to eat "real" food with ingredients that are "closest to the way you might encounter them at their source."[1] But when you get down to it, all food is processed. Hazardous chemicals and industrial machinery certainly play their parts, but even the crudest ingredients require some kind of processing. When grain farmers harvested barley ten thousand years ago, they used stones to grind the grain into flour. That's processing. And so is washing and chopping the lettuce you picked from your garden before you toss it in a salad. It's the *degree* of processing and manufacturing that those who debate quality and sustainability focus on. Some of us will tolerate nothing more than washing our vegetables, while others crave the umami of barbeque sauce on Texas brisket.

But no matter how much we desire simple, unadulterated food, the reality is that, if we want our food to be healthy, flavorful, safe, and convenient, we don't have a way around the steps of processing, packaging, and storing our food. Many of these processes are required by laws designed to protect public health, and whether we agree with them or not, these regulations are here to stay—even if technology improves food safety and monitoring.

Ruben is one of millions of people working for companies that are engaged in food processing. Most of these companies work behind the scenes, invisible to the consumer. That's by design. We really don't want to see how the sausage is made, and if we did, we'd observe activities that might seem inhuman and industrial, pretty much replacing the face of that friendly pig farmer with images of the machinery and slime involved in Ruben's operation. When we imagine the way food travels to our plates, we often omit the part Ruben and his team play, in order to preserve our appetites. That conflict between our imagined food supply chain and the optimized food supply chain is rooted in this aspect of processing.

The technology that goes into transforming our food makes it unsettling. Food scientists, after all, design our flavors not from the ground up but from inside the lab. These scientists often see our food as a set of ingredients known for their chemical properties. They are often disconnected from those of us who see food as sensation, a memory, and an experience that is far more social and cultural than scientific. Nutritionists and food scientists are critical contributors to the solutions we seek to improve our food supply, but they are often tone deaf to the desires of consumers who recoil at the unpronounceable chemical names on our food packaging. At Food+City's Food Challenge Prize Competition, we add points for startups that not only created a new food or process but that also paid attention to our five senses. Never mind that a startup had a winning idea for a new insect flour; if it looked unappealing, no matter how nutritious, we knew the product would have trouble in the marketplace. Food processing and packaging must improve and preserve flavor, texture, smell, and—when it comes to insects—it must minimize the sound of crunching chitin.

We want better stories about our food—ones that preserve the human touch while benefiting from food science and technology. We know more about our food now, and we are ready for a smarter discussion about how to use technology to make our food better, safer, and knowable. Food scientists are getting the message, and at the annual conference of the Institute of Food Technologists, more than twenty thousand attendees display natural additives, often making food feel and taste more authentic (whatever that means). We could fall back on Jean Anthelme Brillat-Savarin, a nineteenth-century French gastronome who described our sense of taste as that ". . . which enables us to distinguish all that has a flavor from that which is insipid." But what tastes "insipid" to a Texan may be considered too spicy by the French. We should be wary of developing technically and scientifically "good" food without considering taste: our sensory and cultural connection to what makes us human.

The language used within the food industry adds to the lack of understanding of food processing. And that language influences our attitudes about food and its march into our digital world. (Dan Jurafsky's 2015 book, *The Language of Food: A Linguist Reads the Menu*, contains an insightful discussion about the way language reflects our relationship to food.) Describing food as "manufactured" instead of "produced" or "made" can be fatal to its consumer appeal. Using scientific terms to describe food also makes us gag. Imagine if we looked at an ingredient label affixed to a banana and read the following: Water (75%), sugar (12%), glucose, fructose, sucrose, maltose, starch, fiber, amino acids, and so on, to describe its ingredients. Not so appealing. So as we introduce the language of engineering into our digital food processing and packaging world, we need to be aware that our attitudes may need some adjustment. We want more transparency about the food supply chain and these intermediate steps, but are we ready for the information?

Ruben knows what goes into his sausages. He is a food scientist by training and has spent twenty-five years in the meatpacking business. He led me to a chilled meat processing room where we found stainless steel tables piled high with pig carcasses already cut into quarters and medium cuts. Workers had hefted these carcasses off the meat hooks inside a small truck that had been backed into the processing room. Occasional grunts revealed that this move took quite some physical effort, even for the stocky workmen. A group of human muscles heaving a group of animal muscles.

Ruben oversees a dozen men, clad in white suits and hairnets, who are bumping bags of pork, ham hocks, and trotters against each other, flashing sharp knives and tossing offal into brimming buckets beneath the tables. The working space is clean, constantly rinsed by water and cleaning fluids, but at some point Ruben will need more cutting tables, buckets, and meat processors to deal with increasing demand for Argentinian pork. Cheek to jowl, there's no room to move without jostling the man cutting next to you.

After watching the choreography required to empty the small truck and prepare meat for processing, we wandered upstairs where the sausage takes shape. Workers in pristine whites, boots, and hairnets swung into action, sliding trays of cut-up pork meat into the jowls of the steel meat grinder. From a room containing buckets of spices come the seasonings that will be mixed into the ground pork, including carmine. The natural red coloring for some of the popular red sausages, carmine comes from the same bugs used to make cochineal, the deep red, natural dye we used to color sheep wool on our farm. One worker pours in the spices and dye, mixing the meat with a large shovel. Steel tubs of ground pork become seasoned chorizo, some batches red and others not.

Meanwhile, on another stainless-steel bench, workers slip a casing— made, in this case, of pig intestine—onto a sausage filler, which opens the casing to enable the sausage meat to fill the tube. Ruben's workers slip the stuffer into the casings with lightning speed, inching up the casing while extruding pork meat into the tube as the next worker spins off lengths of string, tying the filled casing in increments of six to seven inches.

Aside from food processing, but still very connected, are the activities of packing and storing food. All lie in the middle of the food supply chain where raw materials transform into food products that are packaged and stored until they reach us. At the heart of this chapter are the four ingredients we cited earlier: trust, reliability, adaptability, and technology. When it comes to processing, packaging, and storage, trust looms as an essential ingredient.

These processing activities directly relate to how our food tastes, whether it lasts long enough to reach our plates, and whether it's safe to eat. They also directly impact the amount of food waste we generate. If we don't like the taste, if it's unsafe to eat, or if it spoils or is damaged in transit . . . all these failures lead food to the landfill.

The Human Side of Food Processing

You could argue that Ruben is an integral part of the industrialized food system, but you'd only be partly right. Though the human side of these activities is critical and may not be easy to automate yet, it does seem likely that Ruben and his team will eventually be replaced—by robots. The digitization of our food system begins on the ground with hardware and software that provides "precision agriculture." But it gets into high gear in when it comes to processing, packaging, and storing our food. Are humans on their way out of our food supply chain? Most likely, but only in the areas that require repetitive, physically demanding work that would benefit from more control over food and human safety.

Ruben likes his work, he says, and it provides him with more than just a job. While we were visiting one of his pig farmers, three hours away, I got a chance to know Ruben outside of his managerial role at the meat processing shop. During one long stretch of Argentinian highway, I asked about his family. He paused and then said, "It's a sad story." His eyes filled with tears as he drove, and he recounted how his wife passed away a week after giving birth to his now two-year-old daughter. His job, he confessed, was the only thing that held him together, providing one place in his life that remained unchanged, a distraction from the turmoil and a place to find solace and connection.

The human side of industrialized food processing surfaced in that moment. Ruben isn't alone in his emotional connection to his job. Globally, food processors are often immigrants who see their work as a stabilizer and, at a minimum, a means for survival in their new countries. While the gears that drive the machinery matter, the soft parts of the system's underbelly are the human beings that drive the food system.[2] While humans have always been essential in the processing system, the repetitive and labor-intensive jobs are increasingly automated as more science and technology enters the chain. How will workers like Ruben adapt to an increasingly automated food system?

In some ways, the replacement of humans in our food supply chain may be a good thing from the perspective of the safety and health of this workforce. Since Sinclair Lewis and Rudyard Kipling documented the humans working in American slaughterhouses, we have become increasingly aware of poor working conditions in many of the fields and factories that bring us our food. Immigrant farm workers, meat processors, truck drivers, and warehouse pickers have worked in conditions that fail to meet our contemporary expectations for work and the treatment of our fellow humans who make our food.

Automated fillers, trained to know more about filling casing than any humans performing the task today, will eventually replace Ruben's crew at the casing machines. Is this a good thing? One wonders what people like Ruben will do after the robots arrive. He is content with his work, but many others aren't and may be replaced by robots and other technologies. We should be helping these individuals develop the skills to move into redefined jobs or maybe entirely different jobs. More work is needed to consider the future of work. Consulting firms such as McKinsey are weighing the impact of this emerging new workforce and predict that while the Rubens in our global food system may lose their jobs, they will find opportunities in new jobs, some not entirely imagined as yet. These new jobs will pay more and require new skills. Previous technological revolutions point to this evolution of old jobs to new jobs requiring new skills. The transition, though, will be messy, requiring new educational platforms and the ability to move quickly as we adapt our existing academic institutions.

When robots assemble our food, will we be able to taste the difference? Maybe not. And it may be that we will overlook a more mechanized, engineered food system as a tradeoff for greater transparency and food safety, less environmental impact, and improved labor practices.

The Food Scientists

Whether we like hearing about it or not, the truth is that ingredients we need to consume for our health often taste bad or have a yucky feel in our mouths, so food scientists have come along to enhance healthy food to make it palatable. Increasingly, food companies are replacing synthetic additives with natural ingredients so that we continue to want to consume tomato sauce, for example.

Flavor is critical. Have you eaten one of those nutrition bars that is packed with healthy ingredients? Do you savor the sticky, chalky texture, the specious caramel, chocolate, strawberry flavor that settles onto your palate for hours afterward? Me neither. Flavor scientists have tried to make an appetizing nutrition bar for decades. Their success, of course, hinges on flavor. And food processing, packaging, and storage all influence flavor. Processing is just the first stop on the path to the sensation Doritos calls a "party in your mouth."[3]

How would you feel if you ordered an ice cream cone and, instead of the smooth, creamy texture you know and love, you were handed a chunky glob of ice crystals? What you don't want to know is that your ice cream looks and feels the way it does because we add carrageenan (a linear sulphated polysaccharide found in red seaweed) during processing. The thought may turn your stomach, but without the carrageenan, so would your ice cream. These seemingly contradictory values—natural versus unnatural, seaweed from the ocean, and chemical additives—create distrust and doubt about any interference in the native state of what we eat. And most of the additions occur elsewhere, out of sight, obscuring our knowledge of the process.

One additive that has become a reviled ingredient in our food is sugar. Food scientists who are responding to consumers' concern over sugar in their diet are fiddling with the chemistry of food to create sweetness with less sugar, both artificially and naturally. How do we feel about this? The mash-up of our health, convenience, safety, and general personal values around technology and food creates a cognitive dissonance that will only be amplified when we use more technology in the making of our food. Like making meat in a petri dish, these scientific, technical approaches to food straddle the line between our desire for simple, pure, and healthy food and that yearning for convenience that has inspired us to accept more tech in other parts of our lives.

Some processing entails adding micro-ingredients to enhance the healthful attributes of our food. Food manufacturers add vitamins to bread flours that were stripped from the grain when the bran was removed. Consumers who prefer white bread still need the vitamins, so they are added back in. We find this ironic, if not exasperating: nature produces the optimum package of vitamins, and humans remove them then add them back in. It's one of those pesky paradoxes that lurk in our food supply chain and make its improvement complicated. Our consumer preferences sometimes move us in the wrong direction when it comes to simple, clean food. For centuries, white bread has been considered refined, a sign of civilized eating—not the coarse bread of the poor. Why do you think that brown loaf in the bakery is still called "peasant bread"?

Pickles are a good example of how all these intervening steps roll in the food supply chain. They begin as cucumbers, then they're combined with ingredients, such as sugar, salt, vinegar, and maybe turmeric and alum for color and shelf life. Large stainless steel vats filled with salt and water brine the cucumbers. Blanchers are vats of boiling water used to conserve flavor and appearance. Slicing the pickles before canning settles them in vinegar and other spices and makes room for more pickles in the can or bottle. Seamers attach lids to the cans that pass through a pasteurizing process, and caps go on bottled pickles before pasteurizing. All these processing and packing processes are just for a simple pickle.

Pizzas, too, as we've learned, involve multiple supply chains that incorporate similar additives and technology. Each step of these processes can use improvement, and folks in related industries are finding ways to include fewer and more natural additives while keeping the food in its simplest form for human consumption. We understand this even while our current quick stop grocery stores are bulging with processed snacks that defy definition. The plastic-wrapped, cream-filled croissant I saw in a convenience store on a pit stop during a recent road trip combined all the worst nightmares about food in one glance. Those croissants sit way outside the conversation in this book about improvements to our food system, but we should aim for a future when they, too, can exist with fewer and more natural ingredients. Let's hope.

But processing for health isn't all about unnatural additives. Fire chemically transformed food into nutrients at least twelve thousand years ago, when baking bread turned grain into a digestible source of carbohydrates. Heat breaks down raw ingredients, making proteins and carbohydrates more palatable for humans. It also makes some ingredients that would otherwise be toxic safe to eat. Like cassava—which releases a form of cyanide if not properly processed and cooked—and kidney beans. In addition to heating, grinding, extruding, fermenting, smoking, and even soaking make our food more digestible and palatable. Even the process of shelling makes peas digestible by minimizing the insoluble fiber our bodies need to break down—just another example of how our food supply chain ingrains technology as a way of bringing food to our plates.

Fermentation is another way to transform ingredients to make them more digestible. By observing the natural process of fermentation brought on by bacteria, we have discovered bread, wine, beer, and cheese making. Olives would be unpalatable if it weren't for the lye used in the fermentation process. About 4,000 years ago, Sumerians were known for beer making, utilizing almost half of their grain production for brewing.[4]

One of the key reasons food is processed and packaged is to extend its lifetime, ensuring it remains safe to eat from the time it leaves the field to the time it reaches our plate. Unless we were willing to live next door to our farmers or grow our own food and consume it right after harvest, our unprocessed food would be wasted. Anything that can be done along the supply chain to extend the time a food product or ingredient is viable increases the revenue potential and decreases food waste.

Life extenders include additives such as salt, environmental controls such as heating and cooling, and packaging and storage technologies. For example, the arrival of canning and pasteurization technology in the nineteenth century extended the life of many perishable foods. Our pickle is a picture of life-prolonging processes.

Preservation techniques often get a bad rap, and we frequently find ourselves scanning grocery shelves for food that is "free from added preservatives." But not all preservatives are unnatural. Salt, which likely brings to mind that blue package from Morton, featuring the young girl under a yellow umbrella, has been valuable as a preservative and sanitizer at least since Biblical times. Ice, too, is a valuable—and natural—shelf-life extender, as anyone who's ever filled up a cooler with hot dogs and burger patties to take to a cookout can attest. (Granted, the technology that keeps our freezers at the right temperature involves chemical processes that could stand improvement, but that's a story for another day.)

Shelf life doesn't just refer to the shelves at the grocery store or in your pantry. It's about keeping food consumer-ready during its journey to our plates—and at every stop along the way. This means ensconcing it in bulk packages such as sacks, bags, and kegs, and storing it safely in holding points—including roadside pallets in the field, warehouses and distribution centers, shipping containers, silos, and even caves—between each leg of the journey. But the big idea is that shelf life relates to food safety, which builds trust between consumers and producers.

And the failure to produce safe food leads to a breach in that trust, causing no end of troubles for food companies. Chipotle may never fully come back from its *E. coli* outbreaks. Beginning in 2013, food safety breaches caused the company's sales to decline. Although recovering, the company has continued to have food safety problems, leading to such jokes as "You can't spell Chipotle without *E. coli*." While they usually remain in business, food companies that experience food safety problems take years to reestablish trust between their brands and their consumers.

There's another way to eliminate the processing and packaging required to extend shelf life. The alternative is to shorten the distance between the production and consumption of food, and the local food movement's greatest impact might be the removal of any transformation of food for the purpose of extending shelf life. And with the effort to move food production closer to us, shortening the distance and time it takes to reach our tables, shelf life may not be as critical. With the increased speed of delivery (see Amazon Fresh, and 7Fresh in China), the arrival of food to our plates within twenty-four hours of harvest may become the norm. Still, even local food producers would like a little leeway in their delivery schedules, and the grocery stores can sell more food if it's on the shelf. One day lost on the shelf equates to lost revenue. The need to preserve and protect our food over the time required to travel long distances won't disappear, but it may be revised to minimize additives and wasteful packaging between the pasture and our plates.

The proximity of processing to storage facilities and production sites can influence shelf life. The co-location of breweries with bakeries indicates a co-evolution of those two foods and their associated transformation by fermentation. If a rancher has to transport his steers hundreds of miles to a slaughterhouse, he may end up delivering stressed, dehydrated stock after months of careful husbandry. A dairy farmer will pay more to transport tanker cars of milk to a processor over a long distance than he might if he delivered powdered milk. And a truckload of lettuce will certainly expire if it sits too long in traffic. Most efforts to increase shelf life are rooted in food processing and preservation.

The Convenience Factor

The proximity of our food sources to our plates influences how we process our food and our proclivity for convenience. Ever tried to buy a bushel of bananas or a tank car of milk? Packaging allows us to break down bulk food into bite sized, or at least personal, quantities. While primarily known for their convenience, these smaller portions also limit food waste. The amount of waste we produce tends to accumulate over time, since we often have to buy more food than is possible to consume before it spoils. And food spoils from the minute it leaves the farm, compromising the quality of our food the longer it lingers on its path toward our plate.

We may have perfect intentions to use everything we purchase on a Sunday shopping trip, but by Friday we realize the remainder of our milk has spoiled, the leftover shredded cheese is beginning to mold, and the celery we tossed back in the fridge after pulling off a stalk for the soup has now wilted. One solution is to buy food in stores that offer bulk ingredients so we can purchase just the amount of cheese we need that week. Another is shopping more often and buying smaller quantities. But making frequent trips to a grocery store isn't the most efficient use of time and resources.

Convenient portion size is just one role of packaging. Packaged, prepared foods also provide convenience in the sense that they minimize the time it takes to put a meal on the table. Without prepared, processed tomato sauce, we'd be in the kitchen with a pile of tomatoes to peel, onions and garlic to chop, and herbs to wash and mince. While our first food-reform heroes urged us all to return to the kitchen to make our own meals, the current innovators focus on the relationship of food and technology as it minimizes kitchen labor and maximizes the time we spend socializing with friends and working on projects that we deem worthy. Saving the world, for example.

One example of this is the development of technology for making instant coffee. Sudden Coffee, based in San Francisco, uses a new technique for making an instant cup of joe that matches consumer expectations for high-end coffee. While it seems a bit inconsistent—a product reduced to its industrial form for a consumer who savors the allure of a pour-over made in the local café—this product represents the tradeoff between convenience and authenticity. This trend doesn't mean some of us won't be making our own bread or stirring grandmother's tomato sauce. But only a few of us will be called, and still fewer of us will spend long hours at the kitchen stove.

We want to balance the convenience of tech-driven connection with a yearning for convenience that enables us to foster and enjoy those human connections. We want good, healthy food but not at the expense of the time we have to be with each other. Many of us have already made that choice, opting for a fast food drive-through so we can still make our daughter's soccer match or buying ready-made hamburgers in bulk so we can have a tailgate party while minimizing the expense and time of handmade, grass-fed burgers. But more and more, we'll see processed food and packaging that will bring us fresher, healthier, prepared food at lower costs. Sure, we'll miss the hours we spent in the community garden or at the farmers' market, but we can always go there as an antidote to our technology-driven lives. Besides, our community gardens may become our kitchen gardens, controlled with our phone apps and producing small quantities of fresh greens to top our prepared meals.

Defending Our Food: Packaging

Where does Ruben's story fit in with all this? The sausage casing in Ruben's facility near Buenos Aires is just the first round of packaging for the sausage coming out of Ruben's plant. It will go on to be wrapped in paper at a butcher's shop or in plastic at the supermarket. It may even wind up in a Styrofoam box or aluminum foil wrapper as leftovers in somebody's fridge. The packages that cosset our food pose enormous challenges, since most of the food waste we observe is consumer packaging. To see what I mean, take a look at what's in your refrigerator right now. Yes, the plastic jug of milk, foil-wrapped leftovers from last night's steak, a cardboard carton of cream, paper-wrapped butter, just to name a few items. In your pantry, your shelves contain several cereal boxes and cellophane bags of nuts. For a sobering look at food packaging, take a look into your kitchen garbage can. While we are encouraged not to waste a half-eaten meal in a restaurant, we are also expected to take our remaining food home in a container that will keep it safe until it reaches our refrigerator.

OK, so food packaging is piling up all around us, but packaging is about more than filling landfills or protecting individual servings of your favorite snack. Packages are filled with stories about their contents, including nutritional data, measurements, sourcing information, recipes, pricing, and lifespan. They also protect the contents from harm, spoilage, wastage, and in some cases, loss. Packaging provides portion control, sanitation, and protection from vibration and temperature fluctuations. A good package does all of this and more. A bad package sends food into the waste bin.

Food packaging and related activities in our food supply chain are important to our vision for how we can improve our food system in the future. Since we assume we will produce enough food to feed the world if we can solve for distribution, we need to consider how it will travel, in what quantities, and the role that packaging could play in maintaining shelf life while minimizing both food and packaging waste.

Future packaging solutions will rely on innovation from the material sciences, biotechnology, and food science. Early inventors of food packaging, and the materials scientists and engineers of today, contribute to the art and science of containing our food. The art communicates brand information and messaging; the science adds knowledge of chemistry, materials, and nutrition. Art and science together make the total package.

Cardboard, Styrofoam, recycled pellets, and plastic containers carry our food in trucks, on ships and trains, in bike couriers' insulated bags, and in the back seats of our cars. But packaging, not to mention the knowledge of what travels best in what materials over specific distances, hasn't always had the support of technology, sophisticated materials scientists, or even environmentally conscious consumers.

The history of packaging follows the history of logistics. As military planners sought improved methods for moving their armies in sync with supply chains, they also sought methods for limiting spoilage of the food they did manage to procure along the way. Canning and sterilization were the first modern, military-inspired packaging technologies that appeared as the industrial revolution began in the late eighteenth century.

Before then, packaging and storing food relied on techniques developed in antiquity. Natural materials including clay, glass, leather, wood, and tin took on shapes for specific food commodities, and these handmade receptacles provided short-term packaging and storage as early as 7000 BCE.[5] The Egyptians began to fabricate glass containers at scale in 1500 BCE, and glass began to replace leather and pottery sometime in the mid-seventeenth century.[6]

Taken in its simplest form, food comes in its own packaging: bananas have peels, grapes have skins, and walnuts have shells. The casing process in Ruben's plant—fairly innocent as far as packaging goes—is a skill that no doubt took hours of practice. Ruben set up a small "sausage school" in the corner for novices to try their hands at filling and tying off meters of sausage before qualifying for the big table in the center of the room. Back down in the cutting room, the process begins all over again.

Once we process our food, it needs some sort of containment and protection to maintain freshness and provide a barrier from contamination as it makes its way to your plate. The success of a food supply chain depends upon the integrity of a package. A crushed box, broken bottle, or pierced bag cannot make its way to our plate no matter how well the traffic flows. Packaging defends our food as it battles the elements and bangs along the interior of a shipping container.

Key considerations for packaging food include limiting water loss, regulating flow of oxygen, and preventing loss of nutrients or flavors. Have you ever left garlic bread in a bag with a chocolate chip cookie, only to find your sweet cookie is infused with garlic? Called cross-contamination, the transference of bacteria, odors, or foreign matter is a risk throughout the supply chain.

The material and physical shape of a package is specific to the requirements of the supply chain and often the food itself. Beer and other beverages work well in glass bottles because the contents expand during fermentation. Some package designs address transport needs throughout the supply chain, such as beer kegs that were once rolled down narrow alleys. Packaging also influences handling and storing of food, eventually affecting product sales. For example, the shape and size of a food package will influence how many can be packed in a case. If cases are cumbersome or too heavy for personnel, stores aren't likely to keep stocking that product.

Retail packaging, another way of describing individual packaging, comes in countless shapes and sizes—even for similar products. Consider potato chips: A general store in Maine carries Lay's potato chips, delivered weekly in boxes of single-serving plastic bags. Another company, Kellogg's, sells their own potato chips, Pringles, in a cardboard tube. The Pringles package design was a response to consumer objection to broken chips and the amount of air in the plastic bags. Whether we prefer bags or tubes, those uniquely designed and manufactured food packages are for us, the consumers—not the chipmakers. Before reaching consumers, food ingredients travel in much less glamorous wholesale and bulk containers, like burlap bags of potatoes destined for a Lay's chip factory or barrels of wine on their way to the bottler. These containers are for bulk delivery of food without all the marketing messaging and sexy wrapping. They are meant to endure vibration, shocks, temperature variation, and warehousing.

Food-related regulations also affect packaging designs, from labeling requirements to the size, weight, and shape of food-specific packaging. For example, package sizes need to match pallet standards such as those developed by the Grocery Manufacturers Association (GMA), and Federal Drug Administration (FDA) regulations dictate the amount of air in a cereal box.

Smart Packages

But there's more to consider in package design than what it takes to keep food safe, delicious, and intact. Producers must also consider costs, which are dictated by the weight, size, and shape of a package. Some shippers, like UPS, charge more for the type of bulky packaging required to maintain safe temperatures—an even more complicated request for cold-chain shipments. Packagers are working on lighter materials that will result in less waste, require less fuel in transport, and decrease shipping costs. In the meantime, how big is the tradeoff? How much cost can we save without sacrificing the quality or safety of our food while it moves through the supply chain?

What about those soggy pads you find hidden underneath your hamburger meat? Part of the cold chain, meats require packaging that enhances appearance and shelf life. The pads use food-grade polymer materials to absorb moisture. Some packaging actually removes moisture from produce through the carton materials, and other materials such as IceWrap—frozen sheets similar to gel packs—go inside packaging to maintain cool temperatures throughout the supply chain.[7] What goes into the package is almost as important as what goes into our food. And it's just one more thing that contributes to food waste.

The materials inside and outside the food package reveal more than meets the eye. Nina Katchadourian has an eye for storytelling. She's a conceptual artist who has created stories out of popcorn machines and other cultural artifacts. One of her installations, *The Genealogy of the Supermarket*, was on exhibit at the Blanton Museum at the University of Texas at Austin in 2017. The exhibit consisted of framed faces on food labels arranged in the pattern of a family tree, each image portraying someone that represented an iconic food brand: Uncle Ben, Chef Boyardee, Aunt Jemima, and the Morton Salt Girl, to name a few. The artist arranged and grouped almost eighty portraits to suggest that they all represented one big family tree. Viewers of the exhibit brought their own associations with the food brands and the faces on the packaging. Judging from this art installation, food labels tell some pretty surprising stories. But a label is more than just another pretty face. (In chapter 5, we will show how labels come in handy during the tracing and tracking of our food.)

Food ID

Labels have been a way to identify food in the supply chain since the Romans labeled their oil- and wine-carrying amphora with clay stamps, and trademarks and branding developed from the practice of branding cattle, which began in Egypt around 2000 BCE. Still, it wasn't until consumer culture developed that packaging became more than just a generic container.[8] Eighteenth- and nineteenth- century newspapers in England and the United States illustrate elaborate food packaging that describes the attributes of the contents. These early labels were crammed with information and product claims, usually hyperbolic. Since then, stamps, handwriting, and even spray paint have enabled producers and shippers to keep track of the identity and whereabouts of food throughout its journey to our plates.

The information on packaging for the food industry—large lettering and scannable text or bar codes—is functional. By making food invisible, canning led consumers to request labels and grading systems. Unable to see the contents inside the package, buyers want information. Trust and technology come together in the supply chain when it comes to food. When Henry J. Heinz introduced packed and processed horseradish in clear bottles in 1869, he offered transparency to counter the typical amber bottles that were often used to hide cheaper, unadvertised additives.

The Uniform Product Code (UPC) code, part of the barcode, is just one example of the information you can find on a label. During the 1970s, grocery stores got together to develop a coding system for identifying items as they passed through the checkout stations in their stores. The group developed the UPC label you find on food packaging and even on individual pieces of fruit.

But as anyone who's struggled to peel a tiny sticker off an apple will attest, labels aren't without their faults. Aside from the annoyance factor, one of the problems with stickers is the water loss that occurs when they pull off the outer skin of the fruit, and the potential contamination if pathogens carried on the label come into contact with the produce.

If the idea of stickers on your food repulses you, then you might be happier with fruit tattoos or laser etching right on the fruit itself. The first companies to offer such labeling products, such as Laserfoods in Spain, appeared in 2009. The USDA experimented with marking fruit and vegetables, and scientists at the Agricultural Research Center and the University of Florida came up with a way to use laser etching to place product codes on produce.[9] Laser etching requires a carbon dioxide laser printer and can imprint a product with the brand name and a tracking number—a tattoo, of sorts. The method self-cauterizes the etching so the produce doesn't lose water or shelf life. The technology also eliminates the contamination risk and the tendency of stickers to, well, *stick* to other produce and create a glob of apples or clementines.

The Europeans have been leading the way in terms of adopting this technology, and during a European multistage trail race in 2009, I was offered a laser-etched apple displaying the race logo. But the United States is not far behind. The 2011 Food Safety Modernization Act (FSMA) requires all produce to be labeled, so the pressure is on food producers to come up with a cost-effective way to get the codes on the fruit. The only sticky issue is that tattoos, by their very nature, are limited in the amount of information they can capture.

Those who prefer the sticky labels worry that the tattoos might penetrate the skin of the produce, introducing pathogens and causing the fruit or veggie to rot. Those who prefer tattoos like the low-cost aspect of the technology along with the fact that they wouldn't need to inventory labels. In 2016, the USDA approved laser etching of produce, limited to citrus fruit.[10]

By the way, if you get tired of trying to pry those paper labels off your apples, you can eat them. The FDA and the European Union (EU) have published codes that outline what they define as acceptable standards for edible paper to make food labels.[11] One company in the Netherlands, Primus Ouwel, makes edible labels from potatoes, called wafer paper. The company even produces edible paper money for children's parties. Edible "wafers" have been around since the Renaissance, the company claims.

The future of food labeling and packaging will bring us more recyclable materials, repurposed containers, and lighter, smarter materials. Far from the Roman reliance on terra cotta amphorae, we are now considering ways to eat packages as well as labels. David Edwards, a Harvard biochemical

engineer, self-described biocreator, and founder of Cambridge, Massachusetts, startup Wikifoods, Inc., began making edible packaging in 2014 with
the idea that it would mimic natural packaging, similar to the skin that
protects your apple or the cone that holds your ice cream scoop.[12] Edwards
thinks about packaging in artful terms, collaborating with artists, sculptors,
and other creatives across disciplines to develop new food packaging that
will eliminate food waste. Edwards calls these innovations "Wikipearls,"
and his website uses phrases like "couture craftsmanship" to describe how
his team developed coatings and skins that are edible and artful, yet functional. The skins protect food from contamination and provide portion
control. One the other hand, once you touch a Wikipearl, you've contaminated it just like you would a banana peel or ice cream cone.

Edwards isn't alone. Apeel's Edipeel is one of several innovative new
"skins" that keep moisture in and air out.[13] Other companies are focused on
developing other substances that are both safe to eat and effective barriers
against the elements that cause spoilage. Cellulose and chitin (made from
insects) are among the edible materials innovators like Wikifoods and Apeel
are using to coat fruit and vegetables.[14]

The big food companies have the power to shift the narrative about how
we move food through the supply chain, and some of them are beginning
to change their food packaging, especially those in the fast food industry.
In early 2018, McDonald's announced that it would eliminate Styrofoam
by the end of that year, and by 2025 they expect to use only recyclable and
renewable packaging materials. Other labeling and packaging innovations
include smart labels, see-though materials, and even facial recognition for
fruit and vegetables—all moves responding to the consumers' demand for
transparency that can rebuild trust.

Processing, packing, and labeling food take time and resources even after
all those ingredients leave the producer. Packaged food still requires storage
somewhere, if only for a few hours. We store food while supply and demand
struggle to keep up with each other, to compensate for seasonal and market
price fluctuations, and to help ripen our food. Warehouse are integrated
into distribution centers, and they sit alongside wharves, railways, and air
cargo yards. In some cases, storage problems have had catastrophic effects.
And while storing food should be pretty straightforward, the problems have
been building up.

Holding Patterns

In the darkness of winter in 1919, two firemen playing cards in the fire-house near Commercial Street on Boston's waterfront felt the explosion.[15] An unctuous wave of sticky molasses burst from a fifty-foot-tall cylinder in Boston's North End, and the Great Molasses Flood began. The images in the newspapers were of inundation, waste, and too much of a good thing in the wrong place.[16] The firemen never played their next round.

The reason for the disaster was the buildup of pressure and gasses from too much molasses fermenting in a cylinder that was too weak to maintain its integrity as the molasses awaited transport to distilling facilities in Cambridge, across the Charles River.[17] There, it would have been converted into industrial alcohol for military use. The decaying steel tanks were fifty feet tall and ninety feet in diameter, and they were located between a poultry slaughterhouse and the dock where the molasses ships arrived from far away producers in Puerto Rico and Cuba.

Fluctuating temperatures during a January thaw had left the molasses thick and viscous. The sweet syrup engulfed horses and workers nearby, and twenty-one people died. A nearby building collapsed, killing city employees; the firehouse fell to the ground, killing the two card players and another fireman. Red Cross workers streamed into the area to supply aid, including coffee and doughnuts.

The Purity Distilling Company, owned by the United States Industrial Alcohol Company, felt the repercussions of the devastation for years afterward. As a result, Boston instituted some of the first urban building certification programs in the United States, and businesses in general came under greater scrutiny for lapses in worker safety.

Cylinders, silos, caves, warehouses, pounds, freezers, and pits hold our food until we are ready. These are silent repositories, patient structures awaiting the deposit and withdrawal of caloric energy as it moves through the transportation networks joining our cities. Storage facilities and those that work in them are just as invisible as the rest of our food supply chain, to be observed only obliquely, and only if we pay attention. (A molasses flood wouldn't be their preferred method for attracting attention.) We conceal them through our own acceptance that they are unexceptional, necessary accessories to our industrialized landscapes—like telephone poles, dumpsters, or parking meters.

As food supplies increase, so does the need for storage capacity. So when farmers find themselves the conflicted beneficiaries of a record grain crop, they rush to secure space. When Argentinian soybean production increased from more than 20 million tons in 2000 to more than 53 million tons in 2014, farmers lacked adequate storage facilities.[18] As a result, grain traders had to sell in spot markets, settling transactions in one day rather than benefiting from the futures markets. Storage space is one of those resources that needs rethinking as we move toward more adaptive, distributed food supply chain networks.

Warehouses

Far advanced from early Roman storage facilities, warehouses today operate almost as logistics centers, often providing not only storage but also tracking, tracing, and transportation management. They are filled with pallets, forklifts, and pallet racks. The distribution of food requires a robust warehousing system, and warehouses can hold food in any form along the supply chain, in ambient or cold-chain temperatures and for short- or long-term storage. Most warehouses are outside urban centers because they need lots of inexpensive land and ample access to highways and other transport networks. In many cases, food products hang out in warehouses, accumulating until transport systems (trucks, rail, ships, air) can fill up entire loads, which cost less than less-than-full-load shipment (more on that in chapter 4).

But warehousing space today is reaching an equilibrium of supply and demand. For the past few years, warehouses have been in short supply, driving up the cost and difficulty of storing food en route to consumers. The vacancy rate for US industrial space in 2016 was 6.2 percent. Finding available space near transportation and distribution hubs and producers is challenging. And the basic dynamics that influence the rate and location of warehouses for food are changing.

Food warehouses, like Walmart's huge warehouse and distribution center in Arkansas, often have separate docking areas for incoming and outgoing transport. Some have networks of conveyor belts and sorting stations. If you ever want to see global commerce in action, go to a warehouse and watch the speed and volume of goods moving into, around, and out.

Warehouses are being built every day, but their uses may change in the future. The impact of online shopping, the shift to smaller inventories and just-in-time fulfillment, and the development of direct-to-customer commerce may or may not make large warehouses another artifact of the industrial revolution. They may become smaller and more distributed over the landscape. Warehouse designers are looking for ways to optimize space and minimize warehouse footprints. Prologis, a large logistics real estate company, recently began construction on the first multistory warehouse in the United States, located near Seattle.[19]

McLane Company, Inc., a large logistics company in the United States, has recently built a new warehouse operated using geothermal temperature control and cooling installation and designed as a vertical warehouse. Located in Republic, Missouri, this mega warehouse uses robots and AI to move goods, including lots of food, from bulk shipments to individualized truck shipments. The company has forty distribution centers in the United States, and their vertical warehouses, rising in urban areas similar to urban farming, respond to the need to be closer to pricey urban areas in order to shorten the Last Mile and the time it takes to respond to online orders.

Urban logistics and warehouses are about to be thought of in a different context alongside urban food production and increasing urban populations. Shipments from these warehouses will be smaller and more frequent, requiring distribution centers to increase their routes into urban areas. More "hubs and spokes," as logistics managers call them. This is how we will have larger distribution centers in some areas, connected to a greater number of small distribution centers that cluster around our mega cities. Reflecting computing's move from big central processing units (CPUs) of the 1960s to more and smaller computers clustered around those big CPUs, this new topology for food distribution will remake our landscapes in the next decade. There's no telling how small these micro-warehouses will end up being. You may have one in your county or even in your neighborhood.

Robo Storage

What's more, robots are replacing humans in warehouses, following GPS routes within buildings to deliver ketchup up and down the pallet racks. The increasing number of SKUs in the food industry, along with the need for fast delivery, incentivizes warehouse operators to invest in automation and robots. And sensors and scanners that travel with the pallets and products can now tell a warehouse manager exactly where that bottle of Heinz is at any time. Automation is a tool for maximizing space, and space, after all, defines the utility of a warehouse.

Other changes in the food supply chain will alter the way warehouses operate. VR and AR will assist humans in the location and movement of goods throughout a warehouse. Much of this technology will also apply to distribution centers, which include warehouses. HEB, the Texas-based grocery company, announced in 2018 its use of augmented and virtual reality technologies to train its warehouse personnel.

Maximizing warehouse space through online platforms similar to Airbnb will enable small- to medium-sized food products to find space in warehouses. Some startups, such as Flexe, Stowga, and Sparefoot, are already providing this service, offering the ability for small shipments to find warehouse space closer to customers and enabling faster delivery times for the Last Mile. Finding food-grade space, however, will complicate things since cold-chain requirements are more stringent.

The Predicted and Unpredicted Storage Possibilities

Then there's Amazon, of course, ever ahead of the pack when it comes to supply chain, filing a patent for underwater storage facilities.[20] (This might be the perfect solution for cold-chain storage.) Other companies are using AI to merge data on consumer demand to inform procurement managers about increases or decreases they are seeing in their stores so signals can be sent to farmers that cause them to either slow down or speed up their production plans. This will send fewer raw ingredients down the supply chain that may either sit too long in warehouses or be wasted at the retail end.

Despite the efforts of food companies to produce food that meets consumer needs—if not their idealistic demands for simplicity—there is a lot that can go wrong in this section of the food supply chain. Faulty machinery leads to lost produce, negligent food inspections lead to contaminated ice cream, and a deficit of facilities (and miscommunication between supply and demand) leaves ingredients lingering in overstuffed warehouses far longer than is ideal or safe. Packaging breaks open, and contents spoil. So what does it look like when these middle links fall apart?

The Waste Problem

When all attempts to make food digestible, flavorful, healthy, and longer lasting fail, the environment takes a hit and food leaks out of the food supply network. The FAO reminds us that about 30 percent of food produced is wasted, not to mention lost even before it arrives in our kitchens. Wealthier countries waste more than underdeveloped countries that value every gram of food that comes to the plate. While it's a messy statistic (there just aren't that many carefully researched metrics for food waste), this is ample evidence that we should do a better job distributing all the food we produce. And the concept of food-related waste is complex: food loss occurs all along the supply chain, and food waste results after we purchase and prepare food. Food waste is both organic and inorganic. We fill our garbage cans with food and its packaging.

Organic material can break down or be used for biofuel, and most bulk containers are either recycled or reused within the supply chain. Food packaging is filling our landscape, and we're coming to a point when we just can't export it anymore. For years, container ships have been lugging waste—including paper and plastic from our food products—to China, where it has entered large landfills. But as of 2017, China has banned several big categories of waste, turning away shiploads of food packaging waste. Shippers are scrambling to find countries, such as Thailand, that would be willing to take the waste previously loaded on ships bound for China. As ships wander the global waterways looking for dumping sites, it would benefit us to find a way to limit the amount of food packaging in the first place.

Though packaging waste is certainly a problem, so is food waste caused by post-harvest losses of perishables. And packaging, in many ways, helps prevent that. Temperature control is critical to reducing waste by maintaining freshness, and packaging plays a critical role in that endeavor. Eight percent of all the energy consumed within the food industry goes to refrigeration, but precooling packaging materials so food can be chilled immediately before and after harvesting can save energy. Packing and packing material that allows the required airflow is important. Plastic clamshells, ventilated fiberboard, and mass-transfer-limiting pallet boards play a role in keeping food cool.[21] And more and more of these materials are becoming recyclable and biodegradable.

When food expires on the shelf or gets contaminated through the fault of processing or packaging, it goes into the waste bin. Even the food packages themselves end up in the waste stream. Aside from the energy and resources it takes to produce our food, this failure in the middle part of the supply chain has created a crisis in our food system that has enormous consequences for our environment and food supply. Discovered in the late 1980s, the Pacific trash vortex hovers in the North Pacific Ocean, a floating accumulation of industrial waste, especially plastic bags, many of which we used to carry bananas home from the grocery store.

The subject of waste in the food supply chain is one of the main considerations for a redesign of the food delivery chain. We have evidence that we know how to grow enough food, but not that we know how to keep it all in the supply chain as it travels to our plates. This wouldn't be so bad except that one key difference between a food supply chain and other supply chains is the return end. For light bulbs, let's say, if one arrives broken or unusable, you can arrange a return with the supplier and send the item back up the chain. But since most food items are perishable, food never returns to the farmer; it becomes waste. Creating a lean supply chain for food is challenging since the opportunity to lessen waste is impeded by the fact that food ingredients can't last long enough for a return trip. You can send your plate back to the kitchen when dining in a restaurant, but you can't send back your avocados from your kitchen at home.

Intrigued by all the media campaigns to get us to waste less food, I decided to photograph all my own food waste for one week, hoping that the evidence for just one person could provide a real-world insight. Day after day, I positioned my camera over avocado skins, fat trimmings, and orange peels. At some moment, I felt a bit embarrassed by my photo and removed a few items for later consumption. But mostly, the big lesson was at the end of the week when food began to spoil because portions sold in grocery stores were too big for a single person's weekly needs. Until we can get personalized, timely portions to our plate, we will continue to generate our own trails of leftovers. The idea of eliminating all food waste is likely impractical. But that doesn't mean we shouldn't try.

And yet, there's a piece of the food waste puzzle that we don't talk about as much, and that's food loss. Food loss occurs somewhere along the supply chain before the food arrives at the grocery store and includes loss caused by inclement weather, pests, spillage from malfunctioning machinery, or loss during transport. It can also occur from degradation of food by mis-handling, poor packaging, cold-chain failures, and spillage in warehouses. Leaky sacks of grain, a hail storm, or poorly maintained hoses in a dairy operation all contribute to the invisible trail of food losses that occur long before we exercise our right to big portions.

So how much of our wasted food supply comes from loss, and how much from waste? Surprisingly, the data suggests that the overwhelming majority of wastage is caused by supply chain deficiencies. The FAO states that in underdeveloped countries most of the waste occurs during post-harvest—when substandard produce is left in the field or inadequate technology prohibits optimum harvesting—or processing. Produce such as fruits and vegetables makes up the highest percentage of food waste.

The food left in the field is often a result of harvesting equipment that didn't capture the entire potato or carrot. Sometimes, it's left behind because it doesn't conform to grading standards, such as a carrot with multiple roots. The item is edible, just a little ugly. Or it doesn't meet the requirements for standardized processing equipment or package specifications.

Repurposing Waste

The Bible mentions the need to leave some of the harvest on the field for spiritual reasons, but the activity of picking up the bits left behind, called gleaning, is coming back from its Biblical roots as a form of food recovery—the effort to capture edible food before it reaches the landfill.

Now you can find information about gleaning from nonprofit orga-nizations such as the Gleaning Network in the UK and big government institutions like the USDA. The Gleaning Network invites individuals to volunteer as gleaners. The USDA offers a toolkit for gleaners who want to locate farmers with fields that offer gleaning opportunities.[22] Some of the food gathered goes to food banks, soup kitchens, and homeless shelters. Subscription food delivery services such as Imperfect Produce in California pick up "imperfect" or ugly produce from farms for delivery to customers.[23] The idea of using ugly produce is gaining acceptance as public awareness of the food waste problem increases. Food companies that espouse sustain-able practices will seek out opportunities to reduce waste throughout their operations. We, on the other hand, will continue to struggle to balance convenience with the shame incurred with every toss into the garbage can of uneaten food at the end of the week.

When it comes to sustainability, our food innovators are looking for ways to get food waste out of the garbage cans. One is by turning it into energy. Kroger announced its waste-to-energy system in 2013 for its Ralph's distribution center. Stop and Shop New England, a Massachusetts-based grocery, launched its anaerobic digestion facility in mid-2016. Similar to other upcycling grocery stores, Stop and Shop takes waste from more than 200 of its stores and puts it inside a big biodigester, where microorganisms break down the waste to convert carbon into biogas. This all happens at one of the company's distribution centers, where the biogas-generated electricity covers about 40 percent of the center's electricity needs. Even packaged organic material breaks down with this combination of liquefaction and digestion technology.[24]

Garbage to Garden, a startup in Portland, Maine, is an example of how cities can create a closed loop system for recycling compostable waste. Rather than just composting, consumers in Portland and a few cities in Massachusetts store their organic waste in specialized containers that the startup picks up and processes, either for farmers to use as compost or for biodigesters to use for energy production. This model, which is now beginning to take root in other cities, may be a way to integrate the food supply chain into urban infrastructures. Some cities are now mandated through local regulations to compost all food waste. In France, a law passed in 2016 prohibits grocery stores from disposing of edible food. These regulations are spawning new composting and charitable food distribution systems.

For a big vision, see a group of architects operating out of the Netherlands and the United States, who want to design villages, towns, and cities that are their own worlds—living, eating, and using waste to fuel their communities. RenGen Villages revealed its vision in 2013, to much admiration and encouragement.[25] The idea is to connect all parts of the city in an Internet of Things fashion, using savings that would reduce mortgages for those who purchase homes in these "resilient" cities. The vision is bold, aggressive, and waiting to move from idea to reality.

Imagine that you no longer have trashcans at the end of your driveway. Instead, you pour your waste into your personal bioreactor that generates power to be stored for timely usages. These "smart" homes seem like a good next step in the move away from waste that sits on top of urban designs, degrading and hiding the designer's original aesthetic. James Erlich, the CEO of RenGen, is a senior technologist at Stanford University. He's keen to bring his years of advocacy for organic, self-reliant living to the development of his villages.

At the Consumer Electronics Show in 2018, Whirlpool introduced a kitchen appliance that transforms our organic waste directly into compost. Looking much like a trash compactor, this appliance provides us with a steady stream of fertilizer without traipsing a bucket to an outdoor composter that needs regular care and feeding. But will we relinquish yet more kitchen counter real estate to this app-supported device? It would be nice to see this activity directly integrated into kitchen designs at the outset.

Even the fiber scientists have joined the waste brigade, testing tensile strength, absorption, and durability of fibers fabricated out of food. Young-A Lee explores how to make fibers from food while she's not teaching at Iowa State.[26] The EPA joined her project for converting a byproduct of kombucha production into textile fiber. A company in the UK, Ananas Anam, uses pineapple fiber waste to make fibers for clothing.[27] Coconut fibers, seafood, and insect-derived chitin become leather and other fiber.[28] All this upcycling is a reverse supply chain of sorts, moving waste back up the chain and then back down again in a new form.

As with any of these new supply chain innovations, the cost-benefit measurements aren't really known. Subsidies and abstract values such as sustainability muddy the little data that exists for these new approaches to handling food waste. We might argue that putting more effort toward not having waste in the first place would be more effective than repurposing the energy contained in food. Better packaging and personal-sized portioning might allow a company to receive more revenues up front, rather than investing in the capital and labor required to process waste into something else. We could be right. There's lots more room for research.

4 Food Routes

In the summer of 1968, I lived on a small farm in Cossonay, a village in the foothills of the Jura Mountains, a sub-alpine range bordering France and Switzerland. I was there for a summer language program to live with a Swiss family. More than a language immersion program, the experience gave me a vantage point from which to see how small farms send their harvest to markets.

Mornings on the farm were perfumed with baking bread, steaming milk, bowls of fresh raspberry jam, and a deep yellow block of butter made from our cows' milk. During the summer afternoons, the torpid atmosphere was thick with the aromas of fermenting alfalfa and the freshly slaughtered rabbit that hung from the bathtub faucet. Attenuated rivulets of rabbit blood slowly drifted toward the drain. Working and living on a farm is sensual, a detail that complicates our move toward a digital food system.

After breakfast each day, the family milked the cows, drawing enough cream-infused milk to fill two metal milk cans. Monique, the family's daughter, and I would walk along the road on summer evenings, pulling a wobbly cart with the two sloshing milk cans to the village cooperative storage tank. We'd also take the shelled peas and other vegetables we'd picked that day to the cooperative freezer, all transported on a handcart similar to the one we used to move those milk cans to the village.

Shiny stainless steel tanker trucks lumbered up the mountain roads every week to take the milk from the village cooperative to Lausanne, where it entered a distribution center for a chain of cooperative markets. Buckets of peas, raspberries, and corn lined the village's chilled shelves, awaiting the chilled trucks that transported product to Lausanne. Every day the routine was the same. We were small cogs in the complex machinery of the food supply chain, "intermodal" in today's logistics word.

In some parts of the world, though probably not in Switzerland, the transportation of our food from farm to market moves at the same leisurely pace as it did fifty years ago. But in most cases, our food now moves with remarkable speed. After all, the ability to eliminate the time it takes to send our food to us from its origin is the superpower for our food supply chain. The less time it takes, the safer and fresher our food remains. And less waste results as we conserve energy and limit time on the shelf.

Without the physical movement of food from one place to another, we really don't have a supply chain. In the future, when we can see food as energy in the form of calories, and then as nutritional information, our food supply chain might be moving as much data as physical ingredients. But now we move physical things. And it requires a lot more energy to move energy in the form of calories than it will when we move bytes, bits, and nibbles.

The Network

The whole idea of a food system with its chain of activities across space implies a network of sorts. At first, our network was bipedal, then quadruped as food traveled from the ground to our mouths. We carried it in baskets on our heads or backs. Then we domesticated animals to perform the same tasks, speeding up delivery and enabling us to move larger quantities of food further afield. As we discovered new technologies such as steam and combustion engines, larger quantities of food and a more diversified diet became available to more and more people, faster, and farther away.

The essence of a food supply chain is the movement of energy through a network, from bushels to bytes, first through physical space and then through the Internet of Things and the Internet of Food. New transportation technologies may end up favoring data over things—bytes over bites— and while we can't yet understand the consequences of this change, we know some will be unintended and surprising. The transformation of the chain from bites to bytes is revolutionary. Perhaps as revolutionary as the Industrial Revolution.

But today, we're occupied with sending bites, although there are bytes involved. One person using bytes to transport bites is Annette Womack.

She's a food truck driver. Not a food truck dispensing breakfast tacos, but a fifty-three-foot trailer attached to a chassis. On one day in 2015, she looked out over the group gathered in the parking lot of Giant Food in Landover, Maryland. Coworkers, policemen, and city officials awaited her remarks as she accepted the award for 2015 Maryland Truck Driver of the Year. Her thirty years as a driver for Giant Food has taken her into city streets for daily deliveries. Annette keeps an eye on the temperature inside her trailer, aware that an increase in temperature above the required thirty-five degrees could mean the loss of thousands of dollars of food. She uses a computer to optimize routes and communicate temperatures inside her trailer. She's an example of the bridge between human intelligence and artificial or machine intelligence. In order make deliveries, Annette uses years of experience on roads and at loading docks to provide knowledge about the quality of road surfaces and the best times to arrive at certain loading docks. While she uses software that helps her optimize her routes, her on-the-ground intelligence comes in handy to avoid obstacles that the app doesn't know about yet. Hundreds of software programs are now available that offer route suggestions that will minimize fuel consumption and wait times. Some add tracking and tracing of shipments, and many now provide shippers real time tracking on a cell phone, like your pizza delivery service.

Every day we see trucks similar to the one Annette drives. Sometimes they feature images of the food inside, big brands promising a meal on its way to your plate. They rumble along the highway moving frozen pizzas, produce, shiny milk tankers, or livestock with their silhouettes visible through the slats.

Trucks like Annette's travel on roads that join the global networks moving food from farm to table. These networks keep our supply chain in motion, resembling the arteries of the human metabolic system as they move energy in the form of calories into and away from cities. Trucks join other food movers, such as airplanes, ships, and railroads. Each "mode," as they are called, has its own cost-benefit profile, and everyone along the supply chain weighs in with their needs and budgets. Food delivered à la mode.

Much like computer networks, food networks have bandwidths, impedance problems, friction points, hubs, and energy requirements. In Marco Polo's time, camel caravans created their own networks, both wet and dry, over land and over seas. The networks connected cities, markets, and emerging trading centers while faced with limited bandwidth, forage requirements for animals, and deadly attacks in unfriendly territories.

Even though our networks allow the speedier movement of food, they are still subject to hijacking, derailment, hurricanes, and fuel shortages. We are entering a new stage of food networks, and it will require careful navigation between the analogue and digital worlds.

The routes our food takes to our plates usually include a combination of networks and carriers that make up our transportation infrastructure. The food networks include dirt pathways, roads, railways, shipping lanes, and air space. Each network has its own characteristics and economics, and food logistics is the art of picking the right mode of transport to deliver maximum food safety at minimal cost. First, there's the mode of transport, then there's the distribution system, or how all the modes fit together in order to get food from one place to another. Not everyone has the luxury of point-to-point delivery, and many routes require intermediate hubs in order to redirect specific shipments. Today's networks are sprawling, with hubs at critical junctures. In the future, we may have more localized networks with even more hubs.

Roadways

One of the most common "modes" is truck transport. Think of a road as a two-way path between your plate and a field somewhere. The highways that connect our cities trace the pathways of early food movers. The camels traveling across the Silk Road, the principal highway in 2000 BCE, carried salt and spices along a trade route between the Mediterranean and Asia. That network is still operating today, and China's Chairman Xi Jinping has a plan to modernize it with the maritime path from Fuzhou along the southern China coastline to Central Europe. In the United States, most of the food we consume travels over the highway system.[1] And many of those highways began as cattle trails.

The gas-powered internal combustion engine that put freight on our road network in the form of trucks came only after decades of reliance on the steam-powered external combustion engine. When steam technology arrived in the seventeenth and eighteenth centuries, cargo almost sprinted to market, relative to horse and human power. Steam power and metallurgy enabled railways to connect cities in the nineteenth century, as modern technology enabled food to travel over greater distances, enlarging a city's foodshed. Before horses, and certainly before steam engines, humans could cover about eight miles in a day.[2] After steam locomotives gained traction in the business of cargo transport, food could travel hundreds of miles in a day. For the first time in history, food could move faster over land and sea than by horse, and consumers could get food from farther away at a lower cost.

Rumbling alongside us on the highway, trucks are the most visible food movers. They swarm around us every day as we work our way through the morning traffic. If we are especially early morning commuters, we feel like we're driving through a pinball machine, flipping back and forth between double-parked tractor-trailers.

Considering the costs of transport and the fragility of the cargo, logistics managers decide which mode is optimal. Trucks win when food needs to get to places outside other networks, such as rail and water networks. More than 31 million trucks were moving freight over US highways in 2015.[3] Some are reefers—refrigerated trucks hauling cold goods; others, straight trucks (with bodies mounted to their frames) hauling milk, meat, or pizza dough. Most of the food-transport trucks we see on the road today are hooked up to semitrailers that are typically fifty-three-feet long. You can see the measurement on the outside of the trailer, printed in big, black Helvetica type. Some are refrigerated, some are half full, and many blare images of cheesy pizza or silvery fish being hauled out of a Rocky Mountain stream.

Some of these trucks are specialized to cater to the needs of certain food commodities, such as milk, oils, grain, and produce. Cold-chain shipments require temperature controls, while other shipments simply need a shape that allows easy loading and unloading, like funnels for grain and hoses for oil. One type of truck that relies on reefers is the behemoth beverage truck parked in front of convenience stores, its Jumbotron sides blazing beverage brands. These are specialized for beverage delivery. The person with the handcart piled high with craft beer six packs is often holding an inventory management device that connects customer accounts to warehouses and orders throughout that distributor's network.

Our mouths water during our rush hour traffic jam. We guess at where the trucks come from and where they're going. And we're mostly wrong in our assumptions. These trucks may be going from one seaport to another or between food service distribution centers or from a local farmer's field. The trucks are powered by diesel fuel, and the faces of the drivers are barely visible. Those drivers may gradually disappear from our food landscape. Fewer and fewer humans want to sit behind the wheel in traffic for long periods of time with only seedy truck stops between destinations. And now, some of their freedom to roam is being curtailed, or at least monitored, by the new requirements for tracking and tracing devices.

Getting food to us in trucks requires not only roads and trucks but also logistics that search for the shortest distance between any two cities on a delivery route. The need for a safe and speedy journey relates directly to the success of getting fresh food to our plates. Logistics managers use the traveling salesman problem (TSP) to find the shortest route, enabling a driver to take less time and use less fuel. This is classic optimization, the gospel for food logistics planners, and the foundation for many of the algorithms used by delivery services. Circuit riders, messengers, the post office, FedEx, Amazon, and UPS all have to grapple with the TSP. The computer algorithms that calculate these routes will become supercharged with the integration of artificial intelligence, which will merge real-time consumer demand with routing and inventory.

Trucks with drivers may soon be replaced by driverless trucks, geotagged and connected with smart city-type sensors and trackers. All this optimization software accounts for the details of truck capacity, product handling, loading, staging, production capacity, and consumer demand, all with the end goal of optimizing routing, minimizing cost, and meeting the production schedule and inventory capacity. The programs consider the realities of a truck arriving, unloading, and departing a specific location and account for obstacles like traffic and narrow streets. The software also uses information about trucks to match their constraints and includes "touch costs," which are the costs associated with the actual physical touching of the product.

Many of the transport optimization software programs fit the definition of "process control software." The process software crowd calls the task "enterprise resource planning," so you'll hear about ERP whenever someone describes how they use software to manage their truck fleet, inventory practices, or food processing. Basically, it's software that manages all the processes in a business, and the food supply chain is crawling with it. The growing interest in IoT makes ERP even more interesting. If sensors can collect data from multiple points along the supply chain, the opportunity for creating an even more dynamic and adaptive supply chain is within reach.

In the context of new digital food distribution technology, trucking may seem outmoded, and yet it's an industry that is innovating faster than shipping, rail, and airfreight. Labor unions, tradition, and industry attitudes toward risk slow down the integration of even basic technology in some of these transportation industries. The US law requiring a tracking device for each trucker—an electronic logging device (ELD)—is creating another cloud of Big Data that will reveal friction points through a trucker's journey and likely fuel the move toward autonomous vehicles (AVs). Unions won't take these changes sitting down.

In 2018, the shortage of truck drivers was exacerbated by the ELD requirements that limited the number of hours truckers could drive their loads from food production sites to ports and railyards. Trucking companies may break down long hauls of commodities such as soy beans into multiple, shorter hauls, putting trucking schedules out of sync with container availability and port capacities. No change within our food supply system goes unnoticed.

Still, it's likely that our existing food trucking networks will remain even as AVs enter the highway system. Trucks are still good for last-minute "hot shot" deliveries (those small, last-minute delivery trucks), remote point-to-point trips, and their relative low costs compared to some of these newer options. That may all change in the future, of course. And humans will mostly likely remain in the truck cabs, riding shotgun and answering email while monitoring the digital displays in much the same way airplane pilots have been companions to their autopilots for decades.

AV technology, not to mention GPS and other technologies, has entered the conversation about the future of the trucking industry. Most of the routing logistics solve mundane issues, such as lessening the wait time at loading docks or minimizing what the trucking industry calls less-than-full-load (LTL) trucks. Anthony Levandowski, formerly of Uber's Advanced Technologies Group, points out that 15 to 20 percent of truck miles are empty, paving the way for innovation in loading and routing. And whether the trucks are full or not, they may travel in packs, sort of. One company, Peloton Technology, uses Vehicle-to-Vehicle (V2V) technology that enables one truck to read the behavior of another truck to coordinate the controls of both trucks.[4] This "platooning" of trucks decreases the fuel consumption and increases safety.

Attention to who's at the steering wheel will meet those who are working on electric vehicles that will rearrange our transportation landscape away from fossil fuel stations to recharging networks. What will happen to gas stations when autonomous electric vehicles (we assume the AVs will also be electric) take over our road systems? In 2018, Reebok and Gensler announced a new role for gas stations that would turn them into electric charging stations that provide other forms of human recharging: fitness centers, farm-to-table food stores, rest areas, and coworking and community spaces.[5] More than gas stations may change. What about parking garages? A new space for urban farms?

In 2016 Uber purchased Otto, a San Francisco–based company testing driverless truck technology, and announced Uber Freight, increasing the competition among Amazon, Google, Apple, and Uber for self-driving trucks.[6] The potential for optimized truck routes and loads is fueling the driverless technology experiments. Driverless trucking would change driver compensation and impact the limit on load weights.

All of these changes would impact the other modes of transport, such as railways. And as of 2018, the decline in the number of truck drivers continues.[7] Trucking industry forecasters say e-commerce will increase the demand for drivers, but those driverless trucks may fill the gap if the industry can't find humans to drive trucks the old-fashioned way. And it doesn't help trucking industry recruiters who are trying to hire truckers when the media keeps predicting the arrival of driverless trucks. Already in 2016, Anheuser-Busch used a self-driving truck to deliver beer. Volvo and Waymo are putting driverless trucks on the road, testing software and hardware that will integrate warehouses and distribution centers into an autonomous freight network.

Perhaps on their way to this new vision for our trucking networks, at least four companies, including Tesla, have announced their production plans for driverless trucks.[8] Don't be surprised if Amazon, UPS, DHL, and other carriers line up as customers. The new trucks will take less fuel to operate and in some cases will be electric, not requiring fossil fuels at all. And with the promise of increased power, speed, and safety, these new vehicles will have key advantages over the old diesel trucks. But we're a ways off from delicious ice cream delivered by driverless electric trucks. Just getting the battery technology to keep up with the long-distance routes will be one reason for delays in implementation. And prices for these new trucks are still higher than traditional trucks, so we'll need more of these quiet trucks on the road before costs come down. But with Google and other tech companies on the road to deliver AVs, don't be surprised at the speed and frequency of product announcements. And yes, government regulations will attempt to stall progress, but there may be a good reason for at least some caution when it comes to pitting humans against machines on the road.

But what about the truck drivers? How do they feel about all this?

For years now, the relationship between truckers and the governing bodies that regulate them has been contentious. Common carrier regulations also apply friction to innovation, but truckers have been focused on pushing back against the regulations intended to protect their cargo and their health. In 1935 the Motor Carrier Act regulated the trucking industry, defining for the first time the hours a trucker could work and the types of commodities those trucks could transport. By 1980, trucking had become the dominant mode for transporting commodities, including food, and the US government began deregulating the rates and routes. By 2000, however, the United States had begun to regulate the number of hours a trucker could drive again, electronically tracking the trucks and drivers. But a trucker's life, as Annette would agree, isn't easy, and talk of driverless trucks has some trucking companies and truckers worried.

Since there has been a shortage of truck drivers, there are fewer concerns on a regulatory level. But still, those who drive our food around have cause for alarm. They will need new skills and may not want to make the effort to learn or acquire new certifications. And sitting in a cab as a backup to a computer isn't quite what truckers had in mind. The independent character of most drivers might mean they don't want to hand over the steering wheel or take orders from an algorithm that tells them to make a left-hand turn when they know from years of experience that a right-hand turn is best for that time of day in that particular town. Already, just a few months after truckers were required to use the logging devices, the logistics headlines claim that shipments are taking longer and costing more.

Annette probably isn't concerned about the future of her job, but after her retirement, her company will have more trouble than in the past filling her shoes. And even when they do fill her shoes, they will find that trucks face a changing landscape for food transport. With the politics of localism gathering momentum across the globe, the routing of our food may encounter some new roadblocks. BREXIT, TPP, and revisions of NAFTA in North America may change the way we grow and transport food. It's not yet clear what the desire for local instead of global means in terms of where we source food, but the reconsideration of global food trade policies makes everyone a little nervous about the future of food production and our transportation infrastructure. The trucks are caught up in these negotiations, and they may slow down investments in road infrastructure until it becomes clearer how the supply chains will work within this new vision of local sourcing and nationalism.

Railways

In the United States today, there are four big rail networks that move our food: Norfolk Southern, Burlington Northern Santa Fe Railroad (BNSF), CSX, and Union Pacific (UP). According to the Association of American Railroads, 5.7 percent of US railroads moved agricultural goods, including 99 million tons of food products, from farms toward our tables in 2016.[9] Norfolk Southern sends food in bulk throughout the eastern half of the United States, and BNSF covers bulk shipments in the western United States. CSX, the operator of Tropicana Juice Trains—trains designed to transport our orange juice from Florida—began as a single railroad company called the Baltimore and Ohio Network in 1827. The headquarters is now in Florida, and the company's rail network transports food and other commodities throughout the eastern half of the United States. The UP still moves most of the rail cargo within the western half of the country, traversing twenty states and operating on almost 32,000 miles of railroads.[10] Rail networks in the United States and worldwide will require major investments in infrastructure to synchronize changes happening in every other part of our distribution networks. Freight trains carrying food commodities are always competing with passenger rail service for tracks and other resources.

Following other transport modes such as shipping, railways respond to economic pressure by consolidating. In the case of railways, one way to aggregate resources is simply to make trains longer.[11] Another way to cut costs will be by removing humans. Driverless trains, meet driverless trucks. Tracks designed to handle passenger traffic will still contend with freight as we continue to try to integrate all our food supply networks in a way that optimizes time, distance, cost, and quality. For the present, though, railroads will exhibit their willingness to use driverless trains only for safety and maintenance use cases.

Union Pacific, around since the nineteenth century, has been using tech such as sensors and lasers for decades. Its freight trains, the ones transporting our food, use "machine vision," a complex remote scanner that captures data from moving trains to enable UP to see train defects, order parts, and allow repairs en route without waiting for parts to arrive. Driverless trains are here, and these intermediary improvements may help trains keep on track before the robot trains come. Outside of the food industry, the mining industry is already running driverless trains operated by companies like Rio Tinto, and Europe, Australia, and Africa already run driverless trains to transport mining operations. Plan to see more driverless freight trains carrying grain and other commodities as soon as the labor unions give up their insistence on dictating the number of crewmembers required for freight trains.

Waterways

In Boston one morning, the container ship MSC Anisha lolled against the wharf, kept against the dock by the steady pressure of a tugboat pushing on its side. The boat had traveled for eight days from Amsterdam, and the cranes overhead were jockeying containers on and off its deck. This is what sending food around the world looks like today. Hundreds of years ago, food moved along rivers and canals, but in much smaller cargo holds. Today, shipping food on ships is one of the most cost effective, if not the fastest, ways to get food to our plates. Similar to rail transport, the speed of ocean transport is suited to low-value food commodities such as grains and meat. From 2016 to 2017, the United States exported over 8 million metric tons of wheat, mostly aboard container ships.[12]

The practice of using vessels to transport food over water has largely been known for its ability to move large quantities around the world at a lower cost than trains, planes, and trucks. (See the section "Intermodal Networks" later in this chapter for a discussion of shipping containers.) But these vessels also use the lowest-grade fuel, called bunker fuel, to run their engines and have lagged far behind other industries when it comes to digital systems for navigation, loading, unloading, and tracking and tracing of ships.

By spoofing GPS, hackers have demonstrated their ability to be modern-day pirates, making ships disappear while the marauders capture the crew and haul away their bootie. Professor Todd Humphries, a GPS expert at the University of Texas at Austin, demonstrated such a tactic as far back as 2013, so by now the spoofers have probably gotten pretty good at diverting goods. When it comes to driverless container ships, those hackers won't have to worry about the human crew—only the cybersecurity systems installed on the ship. Aside from the financial loss related to losing shipments of food, loss of life could result if nations are unable to receive critical food aid and food companies don't receive enough food to feed their populations.

The lower costs of transporting food on oceangoing ships are offset by the costs of ocean pollution caused by the use of bunker fuel, lost shipping containers, and general contamination of oceans. Bunker fuel is a low grade, thick, viscous form of petroleum fuel used by container ships. The fuel leaves behind a Sasquatch-size carbon footprint and burns slowly, adapted for long journeys across oceans. Keep an eye on the prototypes launched by the Japanese company Eco Marine Power and the Norwegian company Kongsberg Gruppen. Both are engineering cargo ships that will use renewable fuels that combine solar and wind power with batteries to replace bunker and diesel fuels.

The water network isn't limited to ships crossing oceans. The London Canal Museum sits on the Battlebridge Basin, right next to the Regent's Canal. It's also near Kings Cross Railway Station, a hub for trains moving people and goods to and from the north of England. The proximity of the basin, canal, and railway station weaves together the story of how food distribution hubs and supply chains evolve together. Think of canals as human-engineered waterways that transport goods and people in the absence of natural rivers. Sometimes canals connect two rivers, extending their potential as navigable transportation routes. When rivers aren't navigable, a canal can be a useful substitute, circumventing obstructions or enabling year-round transport throughout dry seasons. Barges have transported food such as grain and wine along canals since early civilizations could produce surpluses. Dating back to tenth-century China, canals formed some of the earliest networks for the movement of food.

Perhaps the best known of those waterways is the Panama Canal. First attempted by the French in 1880 and taken over by the United States in 1903, this engineering marvel was built by mosquito-ravaged laborers as they cut a path between the Pacific and Atlantic Ocean. In 2016, the Panama Canal became bigger and wider through the addition of a super-Panamax side lock and the widening of other areas, including Lake Gatun and the Miraflores locks. Since over half of all the US agricultural products travel through the canal, this expansion will have an impact on the movement of food around the globe. The larger ships, made to pass through the enlarged canal, make it possible to transport almost 200 percent more containers per ship.

The barges that travel the Mississippi River on their way to the Panama Canal carry overwhelming quantities. Sixty of the fifty-foot semitrailers you see on the highway could dump their contents into just one barge on the Mississippi. The Mississippi River carries more food and farm products than any other commodity. During the month of June 2017, 37,900 tons of food and farm products were "upbound," and 824,610 tons were "downbound."[13] Now that's a lot of grain, even if it is moving at a crawl.

While canals and barges may seem slow and low-tech in this world of digital networks, they are still competitive in today's food supply chain. Consuming less fuel than trains, barges and their companion tugboats will continue to play a role in the movement of bulk food commodities to shipping ports around the world. Whether it's barges or container ships, moving our food by sea is more cost effective than any other transport mode because of the scale of the shipments. This is why it costs less to ship Atlantic cod to Thailand for processing before returning the filets to the US markets. Costs of shipping by sea combined with lower labor costs make it difficult to rationalize keeping our food closer to home. The economics of logistics often create these paradoxes that seem outside rational frameworks that argue for drawing a straight line between producer and consumer. Not so with competing labor and transport markets. Just ask your local squid purveyor about sourcing the gangly fare and wait for a surprising response.

Shipping our food may become more complicated as shipping companies consolidate along with food companies themselves. When the global economy falters and current rates interfere, ships and their containers go partially full, or even empty. The economy in 2016 and 2017 created enough pressure on shipping companies to set off a round of mergers and acquisitions in order to remain profitable. One company, Hanjin, infamously went bankrupt in 2016, leaving cargo and ships at sea. At the end of 2016, container-shipping losses were $10 billion, mostly due to worldwide economic instability. Aside from feeling the pressure from the world economy, shipping companies have had to deal with cyberattacks threatening to take down their shipping networks and, along with them, the global food supply. AP Moller-Maersk, the world's largest container ship company in the world, experienced a cyberattack in 2017, stalling ships at sea and shutting down its seventy-six port terminals. Allegedly caused by malware from Ukraine, the attack was a warning to the global food logistics industry that technology improvements need to move faster in order to protect these vulnerable networks. With all this pressure, shipping our food may not be the preferred mode of moving calories across long distances.

Estimates are that fewer shipping lines will control all cargo in the future.[14] With fewer but larger ports, truck and rail networks may travel longer distances to deliver our meals. This means that the optimization of our supply chain may run into trouble when there are fewer choices for the movement of food around the globe. If only one port modernizes or has enough warehouse space, shipments of food may gravitate there and rely on railways or roads to move it across a longer distance to a destination across the country. On the other hand, if the trend toward bigger ships that need fewer, larger ports takes another turn, we may see still another shift in our food transportation network on land and sea. The model of a more distributed network of smaller ships and ports may emerge to complement the economics of scale for commodities with the consumer's desire for local and fresh. Might we see a new network of small, even autonomous, sea and land transport vehicles that can deliver smaller shipments to more discrete locations? Ah, maybe this is where drones drop in.

Airways

One fall day during 1996, a British Airways cargo plane landed at Boston's Logan International Airport with twenty Gloucestershire Old Spots pigs. For months, our farm had worked to locate farmers in Britain that raised this heritage pig breed and would agree to quarantine their sows and piglets for shipment to the United States. While not the normal way for food to arrive, sheep, cattle, pigs, and horses all fit into cargo planes to supply producers around the world with new stock. Those pigs landed and immediately went into the USDA Animal and Plant Health Inspection Service

(APHIS) quarantine facilities for several months before they ever set foot on our farm.

Thankfully, our food usually arrives at its destination much faster than those pigs. Because cargo planes and related courier services can deliver food just in time, airfreight can do without expensive warehousing services and eliminate the extra handlers that might add risk to the supply chain.

But this high-speed, high-value network wasn't always an option for sending food to cities. Aside from a 1910 shipment of silk between two cities in Ohio, air cargo's history began with mail.[15] As with many other inventions, World Wars I and II brought improvements to air technology; the Berlin Airlift in 1948 brought food and other aid to West Germans after the Soviet blockade.[16] US planes landed every forty-five seconds at one point, delivering 2.4 million tons of food.[17] During the 1970s, air courier services began to change the structure of door-to-door airfreight. Three individuals (Dalsey, Hillblom, and Lynn) started DHL, and Fred Smith founded FedEx.

Similar to the shipping industry, the health of the airfreight business reflects the overall health of the global economy. According to Boeing's air cargo forecast, worldwide air cargo only grew 1.9 percent in 2015.[18] In that year, the global economy grew about 2.7 percent and has continued to expand in response to the rapid growth of e-commerce.[19]

Today, parcel carriers commonly ship food in single shipments. Food gift boxes and frozen or cold-packed food require some sort of special handling that a parcel carrier or courier can perform. While some airlines carry both passengers and cargo, there are dozens of all-cargo airlines. BAX Global, for example, and UPS, DHL, and FedEx all have their own cargo planes. These couriers, just like all those bike couriers and food delivery services, are in the business of getting fragile, perishable food to you fast.

You pay for that speed, of course. The World Bank estimates airfreight is about fifteen times as expensive as cargo shipped on a container ship, and air cargo planes are as affected by fuel costs as any of the other carriers of our food. When fuel costs go up, so do our food costs. Generally speaking, air transport is most economical for high-value commodities. Sushi, for example, which retails at a much higher price than catfish. Other examples include Scottish salmon and Turkish cherries. But time has value, so while nobody wants to ship corn in an airplane under regular circumstances, if your Michelin chef needs it for that night's menu, you've got a different story. Even with drones and blimps, airfreight will likely always be an option for high-value cargo that requires high-speed delivery over long distances. Digital trackers, sensors, Big Data, and blockchain technologies are all moving into all these transport carriers. Sentry 400 Flightsafe is just one of the products that traces the temperature, location, and movement throughout the air-freighted food system.[20]

Intermodal Networks

Our cities and ports are connecting points for all food transport vehicles, and most of our food arrives on our plates through a combination of at least two of these transport modes. Intermodal transport, as it's called, is the interconnected network that handles food and carrier vehicles in their many forms.[21] These networks are an obvious, physical connection point between farms, markets, and plates. Our food frequently travels throughout the world using a combination of transportation networks, and it moves from mode to mode in shipping containers.

Driverless by design, shipping containers, developed by Malcom McLean during the 1950s and 1960s, transformed how food moved on ships, trucks, and railroads. Shipping containers transport 70 percent of what we eat every year, and they account for over half of *all* seaborne cargo.[22] There are about 20 million shipping containers in the world, and about 6 million of them are riding around on cargo ships.[23] Not all of these are filled with food, since the containers required for shipping perishables are specialized and costly.

Approximately 5,000 container ships are in the water taking our stuff around the world, and now a container ship can carry over 21,000 TEUs. (TEUs are "twenty-foot equivalent units," and you'd need a train forty-four miles long to transport just 12,000 of them.[24]) Shipping containers comply with numerous international safety standards and specifications so they can move on and off ships, trucks, and railcars. They have to withstand shipping slings, hooks, and forklifts, not to mention the weight of other containers stacked on top of them. Above decks, containers live in stacks of four, and below decks, stacks of nine lock into a system of metal guides, tie downs, and stack holders so the loads won't slop back and forth, potentially knocking a ship off balance.[25] Lightweight containers go on the top, with heavy ones on the bottom. The internal capacity of each is a little over one thousand cubic feet, and forklift "pockets" give operators slots for lifting the containers.

The idea of loading food into a box for storage and shipping purposes appeared during the late nineteenth century in Europe, where railway companies searched for a way to eliminate the time and labor costs of loading and unloading railcars. Breakbulk cargo, the practice of shipping items individually, sack by sack, or barrel by barrel, was the common method of transporting food at the time. Putting a group of items together in a box saved time, as it meant only the box had to be moved. In the United States, railroads began using steel containers that sat on railcars during the 1920s. Trucks had become the new threat to railways, and containers promised more freight at lower costs. Now trains, trucks, and ships carry shipping containers.

The general supply and location of shipping containers matters when considering the cost and time it takes to move food from one port to another. Containers, like ships, have their own supply and demand dynamic that influences freight rates and timing. In the case of soybeans, changes in market demand can place pressure on the location of containers. During the last few years, increasing demand in the United States for products from Asia led to the decision by shippers to transport soybeans in ships destined for Asia from Latin American ports to the United States. The ships are then sent on to Asia so they can return full of Asian products for the US market. This eliminates the "backhaul" of empty containers that shippers try to avoid. The reefer and container shortage appears in other forms, too, such as the increase in offloading of reefer containers to trucks that can distribute perishables to more locations than railways. This development puts even more pressure on the trucking industry.

Today, the containers are getting smarter and trackable. Shippers can control temperature and humidity levels so fruits and vegetables can be stored in optimal conditions to prevent spoilage (a dry cargo container withstands temperatures from –40 to 158 degrees Fahrenheit[26]), and US customs officers use x-ray scanners to see the contents of containers, eliminating the need to break the seals and to expose the contents to contamination.

Coffee storage is particularly risky because of the probability of condensation inside a container. Imagine a precious cargo of coffee beans underneath a steady flow of water droplets from the ceiling. Since coffee is grown in tropical climates, the humidity at the shipping ports is usually greater than at the receiving ports, creating a dew point differential that causes condensation within the container. Coffee containers use a dry bulk liner that protects the beans from some of the moisture absorption created by condensation. The liners attach to the interior walls of the container before the beans are blown in.[27]

Food scientists and geneticists design raw materials for life in shipping containers, rather than designing the containers for the materials. "Cargo rice," as the logistics people call it, is a blend of white rice and paddy rice, which is simply rice that is unprocessed and still covered by "glumes" (the leaves that cover each grain, not the hulls themselves). This blend provides stability for the rice because, as the paddy rice expands, it sheds its glumes and creates interstitial spaces that allow the grains to breathe instead of glomming onto each other, rotting the rice. Under dry conditions, rice keeps for up to a year, but if one of those containers springs even a tiny leak, its contents won't make it beyond twenty days.

It may come as a surprise to some food producers that shipping containers actually have cryptoclimates (similar to microclimates) inside.[28] Shippers have dealt with temperature control in the past by using ice, salt, and different types of packing material for insulation. And the growth of organic produce has only added to the need to get perishables into cold storage as an alternative to additives for extending shelf life.

The outside and inside temperatures of a container are constantly battling it out. A container may pass through multiple climates during a journey and must compensate by modulating internal temperatures as a result. Not only does the location make a difference, such as the arctic and the tropics, but the time of day and the season also influence the external temperatures.

But the containers are designed to win that battle. The broad surfaces of the steel box help radiate and maintain the temperature. Each surface of the box reacts to the outside climate in different ways: rain dumping cool water on the top or strong winds circulating underneath a box impacts its internal temperatures. Even the color of a container can impact the effects of external conditions.[29]

Some containers, called "Porthole" containers, can maintain cool temperatures because the walls are insulated, and the container is sometimes precooled before shipping. However, the contents' respiration can contribute to a general warming inside the container. These containers are also at risk of condensation since they rely on natural control of that pesky dew point.

If a container is stuck outside a transport vehicle without power, clip-on generators can save the day—and the shipment. Most shippers require that food cargo be cooled before loading onto a transport vehicle, car, or ship, which makes sense since it would do no one any good for a shipment of strawberries to endure repeated heating and cooling throughout transit.

Of course, refrigerating a shipping container causes an increase in technology and cost. Reefers maintain a constant weather type for the duration of any shipment, even when the outdoor or ambient temperature is as high as 122 degrees Fahrenheit. To do so requires insulated walls, temperature monitoring systems, and the storage and use of refrigerants. Fans, air exchangers, sensors, and motors all work together to keep temperatures in the range required for specific perishables. And all this consumes energy and releases carbon dioxide.

The food transport business is looking for ways to keep the cost of cooling containers low. For example, Sainsbury's (UK) began using a new refrigeration unit that uses carbon dioxide as the refrigerant.[30] The new technology, developed by Carrier, has been testing the boxes with the NaturaLine cooling system, designed for marine and ocean use, since 2010.[31] Expect more of these innovations as logistics and transport companies find ways to limit emissions and use renewable energy sources.

New developments in port logistics enable transport between ships and road networks to save fuel costs. BNSF has facilities in Los Angeles and Long Beach where efforts are underway to create a link between ships and short-haul railways that could replace trucks.[32] All of this is directed toward lowering costs and carbon emissions while shortening the distance between ports and consumers. This is another link that will use AVs and robots.

Ports are constantly jockeying for freight and shipping traffic. Shippers look at the port's facilities, existing traffic and congestion, the condition of the bottom (available draft), and the port's relationship to intermodal traffic and highway infrastructure. In addition, state regulations, security, land costs, terms of leasing, and labor conditions are all big deals when selecting a port. All of this has to come together for a company to choose a port of call. And these considerations weigh in when it comes to finding the shortest, fastest route for perishable food to reach inland consumers.

Intermodal food transport will continue to grow and become more technically sophisticated as it integrates trucks, ships, and planes. Opportunities for innovation abound: one snag, in one country, will impact the other modes and their networks. A traffic jam delays delivery of lettuce from the producer to the warehouse, missing the trucker who is taking the produce to the port, then the cargo-loading window. Global infrastructures and smarter algorithms will increase the adaptive nature of the future global intermodal system.

An example of how this intermodal system operates is at the port of Houston, Texas. Towers of pallets form walls around the port of Houston, which ships the most foreign tonnage of any US port. The port is really a collection of sites, known more generally as a terminal, that include channels and shipping-related companies near Houston and around Galveston. Cars, oil, and other manufactured items pass through the port, but so does food.

Port Houston serves the Southeast along with two smaller ports down the road: Freeport and Galveston. It makes sense, then, that the Houston-Galveston area is also a major rail hub, with five rail freight yards. Combine this with 422 miles of interstate and other highways, plus 755 miles of other principal arterial roads, *plus* three airports in the Greater Houston area, and you have the perfect intermodal transport hub . . . for now. Of course, the share of each form of transport isn't equal—in 2003, the lion's share of transport into and out of Houston was trucking, which accounted for 49 percent of all freight. At the other end of the spectrum, airfreight was just 1 percent. Considering these figures though, we need to keep in mind that food only comprises a very small proportion of the commodities that pass through Houston—or any port, for that matter. Above all, Houston has the second largest petrochemical complex in the world, importing and exporting more petroleum than any other port.[33]

The intermodal nature of transport through Houston has been made possible through geographic location, associated infrastructure, and innovations in food shipping and storage. Gulf Winds, a Houston-based organization that stores and distributes food items, such as olives for Subway and pickles for McDonald's, stores and distributes seventy-five to one hundred truckloads of foodstuffs each week. Companies like Pacer own double-stacking containers that run across the United States through San Antonio to Houston.

Ports like Houston are called "load centers," and they have become entry points for food from international sources in surprising ways. A website called Seartes.com displays distances and rates for port-to-port container shipping; should you have some coffee beans you'd like to send from Japan to Texas, for example: to Alameda, 8900 kilometers, 13 days 9 hours; to Houston, 17,471 kilometers, 27 days, 3 hours, through the Panama Canal. Of course, it would seem to make sense to ship the beans to Houston, where they'd be just a stone's throw away from their destination. But Alameda might be a more economic choice if it costs less to truck the shipment to its destination than for it to travel that much farther by ship.

These tectonic shifts in the intermodal network cause concern for both food producers and shippers as increased demand for fresh food puts pressure on refrigerated, cold chain-dependent traffic. The combination of shipping industry consolidation and increasing demand for cold-chain capacity, including those smart shipping containers, creates challenges for the future of intermodal freight.

China is actively increasing its food production capacity both at home and globally, building its new Silk Road, which is called One Belt/One Road (OBOR) and is one of the world's largest transportation infrastructure improvements.[34] The project is a combined intermodal system that will integrate rail, truck, and shipping routes between Asia and Europe. The networks will be able to speed food trade between those two regions while integrating outlying countries such as Kazakhstan. One of the proposed innovations is the use of digital ledgers such as blockchain that will enable faster transit across borders and greater transparency, so we can stop those who now send illicit honey from China to the rest of the world.

The future of intermodal transport will include food shipment modes we haven't developed yet, such as drones. When Amazon became a player in food delivery in 2007 with Amazon Fresh grocery delivery service, the company that had started as a virtual bookstore became a digital distribution hub for perishables. Now, Amazon Fresh is part of Amazon Prime, integrating its perishable cargo with all the other things it delivers.

At the end of 2016, Amazon had ninety facilities built in clusters near gateway ports alongside other logistics companies. But unlike UPS and FedEx, some of Amazon's facilities are airborne. By 2016, Amazon pulled up its roots from the land-based distribution centers to think about shipping centers in the sky.

Amazon employees Paul William Berg, Scott Isaacs, and Kelsey Lynn Blodgett filed US Patent 9,305,280 in 2014, and it was approved April 5, 2016. Amazon revealed the patent, which claims orders can be delivered from an aerial fulfillment center (AFC). Within the AFC is an unmanned aerial vehicle (UAV), really a drone, that will retrieve the item and deliver it to a customer in nearby city. After delivery, the UAV hustles to a "shuttle replenishment location" that takes it back to its mother station, the AFC. Did you follow that?

The same month Amazon announced its blimp warehouse patent, it also tested its first drone delivery (albeit from a warehouse on the ground), delivering an Amazon Fire TV Stick (a streaming media player) and a bag of popcorn in Cambridge, England, using Amazon Prime Air. This drone-based delivery plan will change up the Last Mile in unimagined ways. The online giant is conducting drone tests in countries with less stringent regulations than the US Federal Aviation Administration. These regulations restrict airspace and cargo weight, but they are bound to evolve over the next few years.

But back to the airborne distribution centers: an AFC includes a blimp that hangs well above commercial air traffic at around 45,000 feet. The replenishment center also includes a blimp that flies to and from the AFC. We really don't know if the aircraft is a traditional blimp, but the patent suggests that it might be. There are all kinds of blimps, and several types of gases keep them in the air, such as hydrogen or helium like the gas in birthday balloons.

The UAVs—the drones—can send any number of items to and from the ground, including fuel and humans. Hopefully not together. So the UAV travels from the AFC to the customer, then up to the replenishment center and back to the AFC. Unlike a ground-based warehouse, this hovering distribution center can move, dodging a menacing thunderstorm or hurricane. It can also move closer to areas of concentrated or anticipated consumer demand. The placement of distribution centers in a food supply chain network is as critical as the placement of a hub or router in a computer network.

Say you live in a city that has been chosen to host the next Olympics. Amazon's distribution center could hover closer to your city as the Games approach to distribute goods that support the surge in pizza orders. The blimps could deliver your order in a heated drone compartment, avoiding traffic and parking problems near the stadium. And, of course, blimps as aerial billboards are familiar sights for sports fans who see beer or Coke ads during all nine innings of a baseball game. Conceivably, a blimp-born warehouse may display an audible advertisement to announce its arrival, just like the neighborhood ice cream truck. You hear about new flavors and order from your mobile phone, then the UAV appears from the sky carrying your sweet treat in a cooled container.

Using GPS and inventory managing software, the aerial distribution system will follow your ice cream along its journey and restock items as necessary. Another appealing aspect of the floating warehouse is its potential to cut down on greenhouse gas emission and use less energy, both concerns for food transportation. Forget delivery in an hour; the patent suggests you may get your cookie dough in ten minutes. Meals could even be prepared within the AFC and delivered directly from on high, heated or cooled within the UAV.

However it works out, Amazon and other companies such as Google and IBM, are raising the bar for food logistics in a way that may enable faster, more precise delivery that consolidates all the human carriers of your ice cream and solves the ever-growing traffic congestion issues of last-mile delivery (but more on that in the next chapter).

David King, from Oxford University, suggested in 2010 that blimps would play a major role in international trade.[35] But, really, they're nothing new. The Hindenberg, filled with highly flammable hydrogen because helium was being rationed during the war, exploded over an airfield in New Jersey in 1937, just after the passengers finished a meal of British roast beef. In that era, food only traveled with the blimp to feed passengers. Imagine roasting beef below a large tank of flammable gas.

Blimps, with their potential for flight and freight, have been hovering in our imaginations for decades. A writer for *Boy's Life* in 1987 wrote an article entitled "Will the Blimp Make a Comeback?," suggesting that blimps would, indeed, deliver food someday.[36] It looks like that writer may have been onto something. The safety of both the food and the humans has a long way to go so we don't risk a catastrophe similar to the Hindenberg incident. But whether drones are tethered to blimps or landing in your backyard, the whole idea of intermodal transport is fundamental to the successful movement of food around the globe. And drones, a novel Christmas stocking stuffer a just few years ago, are now at the table for logistics companies in the future. In early 2018, the Teamsters union put the rejection of drone delivery on the list of objections to the new technologies replacing humans in the transportation system. Boeing revealed a prototype cargo drone that could carry up to five hundred pounds almost twenty miles. For time-sensitive, high-value food products, that drone delivery might make sense. A case of caviar may be the next shipment to arrive on your landing pad as the champagne bottles are opened.

Governments continue to push for infrastructure improvements in order to increase safety, making capital available for investments in technologies such as robots and driverless locomotives. But unions, as in all business sectors, will be resisting the replacement of people by machines. We wonder if disruptions in our food supply will occur, instigated by unions, as companies turn to new technologies or new transportation networks. In 2018, Britons went without fried chicken as Kentucky Fried Chicken changed logistics companies in spite of warnings made by the British trade union GMB.

However it goes for AVs, we should see a turn toward a more automated, digitized, trackable food transport system. (See chapter 5 for more on tracking and tracing shipments.) Ships could deliver our bananas to ports that have automated loading and loading equipment operated by robots that load driverless trucks pulling shipping containers that will be loaded onto driverless trains. Just how far will we allow this driverless chain to go? And if we have a seamless, driverless food transport system, are we sure we can protect it from cyberattacks that would stop the flow of our food from cities?

Transport Network Friction

When logistics professionals talk about "friction" or the difficulty of moving a product from one point to another, the key friction they refer to is distance, and "linear friction" means friction that increases over distance. The longer the distance covered by a shipment, the more friction there is. Shipments to and from landlocked countries usually cost more because of the added friction getting to and from major depots or ports. These friction points are where we need to focus our entrepreneurs and technologists. When trucks drive around half empty, or when there aren't enough locomotives to deliver seeds to farmers, or when labor strikes cause ships to pile up outside our biggest ports . . . we see the opportunity for innovation.

Rail transport of food fares better in some countries than others, depending upon a country's political support for the railroad industry, its economic and environmental resources, and its will to maintain its rail infrastructure. Sometimes transportation networks suffer from politics. Argentina is an example of a poorly maintained rail network that had not been improved since World War II. Because political power shifted to the trucking unions, money was directed to improving the roads, not the rails, even though rail transport is more efficient than trucks for hauling bulk commodities such as Argentinian wheat. Railroads are also more efficient than trucks for hauling food commodities over long distances, since trains move continuously over the landscape and don't have the same traffic problems.

Places that have poor roads or impassable bridges add friction as they incur higher transport costs due to delays or damage to vehicles and cargo. While in Madagascar one year, I observed main highways that were in such disrepair traffic could only pass at ten to fifteen miles per hour, doubling or tripling travel time between food depots. Many farmers simply sold their produce from the edge of their fields along the highway. Just because there's a road doesn't mean there's a functional supply chain.

Trade policies, such as those already mentioned between Russia and the European Union or the blockage between the United States and Cuba, cause a distortion of the food supply chain. Farmers can't get seed, food companies can't sell their products, and the financial system to support those transactions is often broken. Currently, private individuals join humanitarian organizations to send food to Venezuela as the country struggles to feed a hungry and unhappy population trying to work their way out of a collapsed economy.

Outside of distance, skills and knowledge play a role in determining where our food travels on its way to our plates.[37] A trained, cost-effective, specialized workforce can move food production in ways that seem illogical. The New England seafood industry illustrates how specialized skills, scale, and proximity to markets can shape the food supply chain. And it doesn't look like the shortest route. Jared Auerbach is the founder and CEO of Red's Best, a seafood wholesaler that operates from Boston's Fish Pier. A relative newcomer to the seafood business, Jared founded Red's Best in 2006 with the goal of keeping New England fishermen fully employed. To do so requires his 110 employees to work around the clock, unloading the full catch of each boat that sells to Red's. His company processes, packs, and ships out the fish to buyers around the world.

Some of the fish goes to China for processing and then onto Japan to be sold at the world's largest wholesale seafood market, Tsjuiki. Imagine the apparent paradox of a fisherman who catches and sells a sushi-grade Bluefin tuna to Red's, only to see it transferred through Logan airport to Japan's market—and then *back* to Boston when a sushi restaurant buys it from Japan. Thousands of miles later, the sushi-grade fish supply chain has succeeded in bringing fresh fish to the table. Auerbach chooses squid processors in Asia for their skills and the cost of labor. At one time, he attempted to find local squid processors but couldn't match the specialized labor market in Asia.

How can that be? Specialization is one reason. Fish processors in China can process fish at lower cost than any of New England's local processors. Squid, for example, lands in Provincetown, Massachusetts, and travels to China for processing for far less than it would cost Jared to hire three hundred squid processors in New England. China offers lower processing costs and a more refined skillset than US wholesalers can find closer to home.

Tariffs and trade wars also disrupt the flow of food. In 2018, the United States began a series of trade talks with its trading partners aimed at adjusting existing tariff agreements. While these negotiations were underway, the announcement of tariffs on US soybeans exported to China caused China to consider other sources such as Brazil. Because agricultural products require synchronization with seasonal growing seasons, just the anticipation of change can cause supply chain shifts.

Sometimes the more convoluted intermodal networks in the food supply chain find ways of straightening themselves out. For almost fifty years, perishable produce grown in South America had to be shipped to ports in the northeastern United States instead of through more southern ports such as Houston. Due to concerns over fruit flies, southern ports had played a limited role in the perishable supply chain coming from Latin America. Northern ports were thought to be immune to, or at least farther away from, the infestations that originated in the Southern Hemisphere.[38]

But as consumer demand for fresh produce grew, the northern ports were struggling to keep up.[39] What's more, the time it took to ship South American produce to northern ports and then back to distribution centers in the southern United States led to increased food waste. To solve the problem, the USDA, which had originally created the regulation, began a pilot program in 2013 to allow southern ports to begin accepting perishable produce from Latin America.[40] The pilot program is located in Florida, where Tampa Bay partnered with CSX Transportation to develop the Green Express freight train for produce. All told, the elimination of truck transport from the Northeast to southern markets will save about $3,500 per container in fuel costs and increase profit margins for grocers.[41]

Another convoluted supply chain may yet get straightened out, in spite of the failed efforts so far. The United States still ships food thousands of miles to countries in need of food aid, even though food policy experts, such as those with the FAO, advocate for developing countries to develop their own food systems so they can grow their own local food supply. When there is a food emergency, it is almost always much cheaper and more effective to buy food nearby rather than take the time and expense of sourcing food in the United States and shipping it.

Charitable organizations exist for the purpose of feeding developing nations, and some countries have developed a culture of consuming imported food at the expense of developing their own local skills and resources. This is both a transportation and distribution malfunction, and it will be interesting to see who straightens out this supply chain—and how they manage it. Former US Presidents George W. Bush and Barack Obama tried, but both failed.[42] Too many old ties keep this supply chain in place, but these old ties are coming undone in recent times as we see transportation, finance, and politics find new ways to operate outside traditional communities and practices. While a change in the way we send food aid around the world may seem like a win-win for sustainability, old supply chains die slowly. US farmers send food aid, and longshoremen load it onto ships for transport to Africa. You can see how these interests clash with the logic needed to improve the global food supply chain. Maybe the longshoremen and agricultural lobbies will be the next institutions to unravel.

Whether or not we see the rationale of a food supply chain, we understand that the speed and cost of transport is key in the food logistics world. Some food can saunter through the supply chain, like corn, soybean, and other commodities that slither down rivers and roll on and off container ships. Other foods need unobstructed, frictionless speed, and they often need jet engines to propel them toward our plates. Alas, to find the sweet spot is our common logistics obsession. Transportation is where all four of our ingredients merge to find the best combination of all the ways to move food, whether on roads, waterways, railways, airways, or a combination of all the networks.

One wonders what will happen when other services replace the humans that drive the Frito-Lay trucks. Will we miss the humans that now deliver our food? Will rural routes lose their connection with the world outside? With all the attention focused on the urbanization of our global landscape, who will be paying attention to the countryside? And what will be left outside cities as they become larger and include more and more rural landscapes? This emptying out of the countryside isn't new; Victorians rushed to cities in order to escape the arduous and grimy life of farming. But as cities agglomerate, they may need reconsideration as either extensions of the metropolis or as their own ecosystems, complimentary to cities, but outside urban systems. Maybe we should consider a landscape that includes a design for the integration of both the urban and rural ecosystems as a codependent system.

5 Food Tracks

Remember Fred and Carrie in the 2011 *Portlandia* episode "Ordering the Chicken?" Dana, a server in a Portland restaurant, responds to Carrie's request for more information about the chicken on the menu by launching into a long paragraph of descriptors for the bird, including "heritage breed," "woodland raised," and "fed sheep's milk and hazelnuts." Still not satisfied, Carrie and Fred read the official papers provided by Dana describing Colin the chicken's origin and pedigree. By the end of the episode, the still unsatisfied duo get up from their table and announce they are off to visit the farm where Colin lived so they can verify all the claims made about his life before his demise.

Even though this episode appeared in 2011, the scene Fred and Carrie caused will be familiar to servers and restaurant-goers today. Today we want to unravel the whole journey of our food as it travels from field to fork, and the market is responding. And it's not just the server that we interrogate. We expect our food labels to provide a full narrative of our food's journey from farm to plate. Last week I held my smartphone scanner up to a QR code on a box of blackberries to see the smiling faces of the family who produced them. And in 2017, OriginTrail, a startup finalist from Italy in our Food+City Challenge Prize competition, began offering clients the ability to provide consumers with stories for ingredients as they pass through the supply chain.

The food industry is hot on the trail of technology that will help the industry, regulators, and consumers know where our food is at every step of the supply chain. Consumers' growing appetite for information about food comes from the desire to trust the food system. As the routes our food takes change, the new footprints will need to be hyper transparent, traceable, and verifiable. There's no greater opportunity to improve trust within our food system than by finding better ways to track and trace our food throughout the pathway from farm to plate.

Why? How has this happened, this awkward moment when the art of dining becomes the art of interrogation? Why are we obsessed with our food's origin? Why is the quality of our food defined by the names and locations of the people who make it? The desire to know where our food is or has been is now one of our greatest cultural obsessions. As Eve Turow explains in her book, *A Taste of Generation Yum*, millennials and Gen Zers want to see and hear about who produces their food and who is at the other end of a food-related transaction. With the cultural turn away from presumptive trust of capitalism along with the desire for more personal connections, they want the food system to become visible and understandable.

The whole concept of time and distance explored in chapter 2 surfaces in the way we describe food roots and routes. And when we arrive at a system for knowing the full routing of our food, we may discover a need for compromise between our aspirations and our pragmatism. We may want a route that is fully traceable and knowable, but after we know enough to trust our food, we may move on to other obsessions. Those who remain obsessed will be those in the food industry who monitor food safety and security.

Tracking and tracing food is a challenging proposition, considering all the various methods and inconsistencies of record keeping. But adding in all the friction points where the flow is even momentarily arrested makes the tracking and tracing system even more complex. In some cases, scenarios for delayed food shipments are random. Some disruptions can't be imagined, so we can't predict them. The food supply chain is full of paradoxes and perturbations

Food Tracks

The race toward complete traceability will intensify before we find the sweet spot for food safety and trust. Now, food logistics companies announce another way to apply the latest technology to finding our food wherever it may be in the supply chain. Tracking our food even before it officially enters the supply chain is just one example of how our next bite may be closely monitored.

Facial recognition is beginning to enter our food system, making the *Portlandia* duo seem amateurish. Go-Go Chicken of China is using the technology to individually track each of their chickens from henhouse to your house.[1] Each chicken wears a tracking device affixed to one of its feet to enable real time movements to appear on a customer's cellphone. The IoT that enables other industries to track goods and services provides the platform for this Internet of Chickens (IoC) that tracks every movement of your drumstick. If you wonder whether your cage-free chicken really enjoyed a daily walkabout before its demise, now there's a way to find out.

The company is confident about the demand for these high-priced chickens. They know the foodie, millennial, and well-to-do middle-class consumers will pay more to see more of their food. And who knows, maybe consumers will consider watching their food march toward their plates as a form of foodie tourism, a way to "visit" farms and meet the farmers. (By the way, it's not just chickens; ZhongAn Technology is working on fish face recognition, and cow face recognition became a reality early in 2018. Yes, really.)

While the idea of virtually meeting your chicken before it becomes dinner may bring a smile to your face, it reveals that some of our news about innovation is complicated by a lack of understanding about what's really going on in our food supply chain. While poultry facial recognition may feel a bit absurd, most of the technology we use to track our food from farm to table serves important purposes in food safety and security. For example, the IoT approach to food data collection and the use of blockchain are combining to address the problem of food counterfeiting and fraud. (See the last section of this chapter, "Blockchain: The New Superpower?" for an explanation of blockchain technology.)

The distribution of our food to our plates is one of the parts of our food supply chain that is under reconstruction, or "in disruption," as our tech friends say. Not only is the pathway changing, but the means of tracking and tracing food throughout the pathway is changing, too. Having both change at the same time could be beneficial. Once the ground is upturned, it's easier to install new networks. But this could also be a time of disorientation and high risk with so many parts of the supply chain under reconstruction.

Not only are so many points in our food routes changing, but they are also losing public trust through revelations about food contamination, animal welfare, food fraud, and lapses in our food safety inspection system. Trust among all the participants in the supply chain is critical. If the chain breaks, or if its integrity is even suspect, the risk and probability for contamination, fraud, or theft increases. To establish trusted relationships among all parties, everyone in the chain must have a good way to keep consistent, compatible records. Yet in practice, our global food supply chain is fragmented and inconsistent.

Hidden Trails

A company's investment in food tracking and tracing technology—and it takes a significant investment—is related to its willingness to share information and its interest in communicating this new transparency. But some food producers and distributors consider their supply chain data proprietary, a form of intellectual property. As they see their business, the ability to source ingredients wisely is the very advantage that makes their company competitive in a highly competitive, low-margin industry. It may be that the culture of openness emerging in other industries will move food companies closer to sharing an important part of their intellectual property and competitive edge: their supply chain and logistics management strategies. But don't hold your breath.

Those who work on feeding armies and refugees need to be transparent to contractors and suppliers all over the world, as they're required to coordinate food supply chains to the most remote cities in the world. US food logisticians share data and logistics infrastructures with enemies to get access to roads and ports. Food tracking systems need to operate transparently so supplies can reach military sites and refugee camps around the world. These food logistics practices are now trickling out of the military and into the everyday supply chain, coinciding with a cultural change around the world now that consumers want to know where their food comes from. And all this desire for transparency could threaten our food security. Terrorists and hackers can see where our food comes from, too. But it works both ways: we will also be able to track down the counterfeiter, the thief, and other malefactors. Transparency is complicated.

Forks and Hope

Lewis Carroll's *The Hunting of the Snark*, written in 1876, is an account of the hunt for a fictitious Snark. Carroll tells his readers that the only way to track down the creature is to use forks and hope, two assets that most of us use to find out where our food comes from. Forks feed our curiosity, and hope is about all we have to sustain our search.

As we've seen, our food's routes to our plates take more twists, turns, detours, and roadblocks than many of us have ever imagined. Most involve some type of aggregation facility, like a distribution center, hub, or warehouse. Some use only a vehicle—even a bicycle—to move food from a farmer to a consumer. When in Madagascar, I observed bread arriving in a small village carried by a young man on a bicycle. He reached into the basket behind his seat, pulled out a long baguette, and handed it to a woman waiting outside her grass hut. Some baguettes arrive through vending machines in Paris, of all places, and others fill grocery stores after being off-loaded from a tractor-trailer. A single food item has all kinds of routes to travel, and now we want to know more about those journeys, all of them.

The Midlands

Before entering the tangled world of tracking and tracing our food, we should look at how the routes we want to see are designed. Some of the routes are direct, but others, well, they seem to dash back and forth all over the map as our food changes hands between big distributors in tractor-trailers and couriers on bicycles.

All these players in our food supply chain—food processors, brokers, traders, food services, and warehouse companies, just to name a few—are middlemen in the system that brings our food to our plates. Today we are seeing a disintermediation of our food system as startups and inventors pick off one aspect of the supply chain and add a tool for optimization, personalization, or other value-added features such as localizing food sources. Like the financial industry that is watching millions of individuals who formerly relied on advisors to manage their portfolios learn to do it themselves using a phone app, the food industry will continue to see an evolution away from middlemen like food service distributors such as Sysco, to apps that find local meat producers who show you the exact chicken you'll be dining on that night.

In some cases today, our food arrives through a route managed and owned by one company. Pepsico owns most of its own trucks and warehouses. Dominos gets us to use our own vehicles but manages the system through its own tracking system. Uber Eats is a more recent example of a combination of food service and a ride sharing company that contracts with individuals who use their own cars but operate using Uber's software.

A continuing mash-up of vertical and horizontal businesses will continue to emerge as food companies send their meals through partnerships with logistics companies, logistics companies send us food, and food companies make and send food through their own supply chains.

A number of third parties bring us food. These include transport companies such as UPS and DHL, brokers, and freight forwarders. Logistics companies such as UPS are finding ways to load more food deliveries through existing cold-chain systems and by feeding customers where they are already traveling. The cargo traveling through this Last Mile includes raw ingredients such as coffee beans and meat, meal kits, cooked meals, and groceries. Food in just about any form.

These third-party food carriers coordinate shipments, find transport vehicles, determine the best routes, and in some cases warehouse our food on the way to our plates. These companies in the food distribution part of our supply chain all work to optimize the time, costs, impact on the quality and safety of our food, and increasingly the environmental impact of transport. And there are advantages and disadvantages of any arrangement. Food services, including restaurants, risk a loss of consumer trust if a food delivery is compromised along the way. Say your pizza is cold or your ice cream is melted. You will think poorly of the food brand or company, not the delivery service that may have mishandled your precious pint of cookie dough ice cream. And consumers are an impatient lot: once they're sent a cold pizza, they may never buy their pizza from that company again.

Distribution Centers: DCs

Distribution centers are in the thick of the tracking and tracing network. They operate as the hubs between networks and monitor the transfer of our food from one source to another. Distribution centers (DCs, as they are called in the logistics world) are a good place to begin to understand the challenges of tracking and tracing. One company that uses a range of distribution formats is Walmart. When I visited Walmart in Bentonville, Arkansas, I saw its distribution center, a sprawling building that consumed the contents of trucks on one end and sent them on their way, reloaded with full loads destined for regional hubs. Standing on the elevated catwalks in the distribution center, you can see across a sea of conveyor belts carrying packs of canned peas and jars of pickles toward trucks awaiting cargo below.

Employees known as "pickers" hustle to snatch items that have arrived on one inbound truck and place them on conveyor belts in transit to other, outbound trucks. Multiple belts transfer items that are shunted onto other belts, moving toward other employees—"packers"—who assemble outbound shipments. Viewed from above, the whole system seems like a representation of nonstop global commerce.

The Walmart model is an example of regional centers that distribute food for large retail chains such as Safeway, food service companies such as Aramark, or restaurants like Cheesecake Factory. By 2017, Walmart had 173 distribution centers in the United States, including those for Sam's Clubs, with a total square footage larger than Manhattan.[2]

DCs are where goods aggregate before traveling to consumers. High fuel prices and unpredictable demand for food in large cities encourage growth of these megawarehouses.[3] The rise of the global economy beginning in the 1980s also created the need for DCs, and the economies of scale enabled large shipments to travel through distribution warehouses at lower cost than the smaller, regional hubs. The larger DCs operate 24/7, enabling greater optimization of truck routes while minimizing driver wait times. We're about to see the disaggregating of DCs as regional and local demand ramps up and the means for predicting demand improves.

Some big DCs send items to smaller sub-DCs closer to cities. But some are smaller, taking the form of food banks and producers that use Community Supported Agriculture (CSAs) to distribute their goods. Food hubs are also a type of DC, a site that aggregates food from multiple producers for distribution in a metropolitan area or region. Some DCs use sophisticated software to match producers with buyers and to optimize routes.

All these activities contribute to the food supply value chain by expediting shipments, finding better routes, and providing warehouses or cold-chain services. The distribution of our food, in its many forms, whether done by a single company or through multiple parties and nonprofits, is about to change. Actually, it's changing right now.

The Last Mile

The last delivery route between a hub, distribution center, warehouse, or even a produce stand and the consumer is known in the logistics world as the "Last Mile." The Last Mile refers to the distance between the last distribution hub and the consumer, and it accounts for almost 30 percent of the total cost of transporting food. And it's rarely a statute mile.

The actual distance of that last leg of the journey to our tables isn't always measured as a mile. It may be as short as the Dominos driver's route from the store to your front porch, or it may be hundreds of miles if the last distribution hub for a grocery store in Kansas is a port in Louisiana. Either way, the Last Mile is the distance that encounters the most traffic, parking issues, scheduling traumas, last-minute orders, logjams, and collisions. Traffic congestion isn't new: Victorians in England complained about the congestion of horses and streetcars. But now, getting to your food to your plate is even more complicated in the narrow, cobblestone cities in Europe and the muddy, dirt roads in Indonesia. And now, it's a traffic jam.

The Last Mile can feel like a million miles for a food delivery truck driver caught in traffic. After an excruciating effort to preserve a pint of fresh strawberries en route to our plates, a farmer may find that the fragile gems rot in the back of a truck on a hot afternoon. And in a developing country like Sudan or in conflict areas in Middle Eastern countries, the Last Mile may be impassable.

Deliveries of food to our local grocery stores or of bottles of wine to wine shops must take into consideration stairs, elevators, fragility of walls and décor, presence of customers in the retail space, and timing. One Last Mile delay early in the morning leads to an accumulation of delays throughout the day. This is a friction point in the supply chain that deserves attention from scientists and engineers who want to solve big problems in our global food supply chain.

Last Mile food delivery has a modern history that began during the late 1980s with early entrants such as Peapod and Webvan. Both came from the grocery business, promising to deliver groceries to homes near their stores. Peapod, a pioneer in online e-commerce, began operations in 1989 and still operates as a subsidiary of Ahold Delhaize. Amazon turned Webvan's failure into Amazon Fresh, and other companies with similar objectives soon joined in the home delivery of food. FreshDirect, which began delivering food to areas of the Northeast in 1999, joined an increasing number of food delivery services. By now, there are at least 150 food delivery companies driving a Last Mile to deliver food to your kitchen. Amazon's Prime Now links you to its own food inventory or those of its Whole Foods network of stores. It seems that there's a rush to get to your door by every grocery store chain, from Costco and Walmart to Dominos pizza and the many independent food delivery services such as Doordash, Deliveroo, and Door-2-Door. It's not uncommon to find grocery aisles jammed with personal shoppers who are picking and packing food for either the grocery store's Last Mile service or for a contractor such as Instacart that is also rushing to cover the Last Mile with its own drivers. So, it's not only grocery to you, it's food producer, food service, and restaurant to you. Cheese shops, wine makers, and mushroom foragers are crowding into the Last Mile, potentially adding unnecessary carbon dioxide to the atmosphere and costs to your meal.

Some of these food logistics companies are occupying bodegas or other storefronts and use them only as delivery hubs. These "dark stores" are sparsely manned by humans, functioning as microwarehouses for a distribution network where humans, robots, or a combination would be closer to customers to enable shorter Last Miles and faster delivery times. Artificial intelligence will need to augment these microwarehouse designs (see the discussion of warehouses in chapter 3) so that each site will have the smartest, leanest inventory.

Your buying behavior combined with predictive analytics will inform the distributor which food products to stock and when. Soon, demand planning will become a priority as the digitization of the supply chain increases its momentum, fueled by the need to manage transport prices in a competitive global environment. Producers will connect through the supply chain all the way to your place and could plan supply so it could more closely meet demand. This can only happen when the tracking and tracing improvements allow for sharing, standardizing, and digitizing of the entire supply chain.

Some food companies have been working on digitizing their supply chains for decades. Dominos Pizza Company has worked at perfecting Last Mile delivery from its point-of-sale systems to its pizza delivery system. For a pizza company, that means getting every fresh-from-the-oven pizza to the customer who ordered it before it becomes a soggy mess. Owning the logistics service is one way to ensure a better experience for the consumer who expects a hot pizza.

More recently, startup companies have begun taking on the Last Mile challenge themselves. These new food delivery services are like the old-school bike couriers, enhanced by apps that connect customers with drivers and food businesses. DoorDash, one of these services, announced in 2017 that it would use complex delivery algorithms to provide customers with predictive, accurate delivery times. This means accounting for the route but also for the time it takes to make each item. The "Dashers" are part of the new on-demand economy and struggle with many of the same challenges as Uber Eats or Postmates. For the Last Mile Problem, DoorDash wants to use data to be a smarter delivery service, learning from experience so it can inform customers when their pizza will arrive as it struggles with the Last Mile hurdles.[4] And to improve the Last Mile logistics, DoorDash began to use both data and a robot to deliver food and predict its arrival, and in 2018 it began a partnership with Walmart to deliver groceries. Other startups such as Favor (acquired by the grocery retail chain HEB in 2018), Instacart, and many specialized delivery services that bring you ice cream, cheese, meat, beer, or all of the above, are all crowding into our driveways.

Other startups are working on the delivery vehicles. Starship Technologies developed autonomous robots that can carry up to forty pounds of food and groceries. New delivery options, a bit smarter than that first wave of food delivery startups, are appearing every week, trying to design a better use of existing logistics networks and knowledge.

The Last Mile is under reconstruction. The scramble for meal kit delivery, delivery meals, and the changing format of grocery stores that will impact where we eat is in the process of renegotiation. Blue Apron and a gaggle of others that are jockeying for space at our front doors haven't yet found a logistical model that is financially sustainable. The concept of free delivery, championed by Amazon and for a while by UPS, is losing traction as logistics companies realize the complexity and costs of delivering perishable goods to our doorsteps. But hopes are high, as are startup valuations. Blue Apron was the first meal kit delivery company to go public; by mid-2015, the company's valuation was $3.2 billion, with revenues of $750 million to $1 billion in 2016. The company's stock was valued at $10 per share when it went public, but in early 2018 it had sunk to $3 per share. Stung by fulfillment problems and hindered by the high cost of customer acquisition, the company struggles to grow. Blue Apron's story is similar to other Last Mile delivery companies, which may gradually become takeover targets for more established retail food companies. Some food delivery services have died only to reemerge with a new business model or management team; one example is Good Eggs, a food delivery service that seemed to be unsustainable in 2015 only to resuscitate itself with new funding in 2018. The newly organized company promises to eliminate the distribution center model for a direct delivery model that delivers fresh food from local farmers in the San Francisco Bay Area. But this is a tough business with venture capital funding on the decline.

One of the reasons for this coming shakeout is that none of the new entrants in Last Mile meal delivery is profitable. But neither was Amazon until 2003, almost ten years after its founding. Most industry observers forecast that no one format for Last Mile delivery will win out. Instead, we'll have multiple choices for how food reaches our plates. On Monday, you may want to go out to a restaurant; Tuesday, cook with a meal kit delivery; Wednesday, enjoy a dinner prepared by a chef who comes to your house to cook; and on Thursday, you may want a pizza delivered. Friday you sit down to a meal prepared at an in-store restaurant at your favorite grocery store. And Saturday night, well, that's a night out on the town.

Last Miles have become a crowded space these days. Seems everyone wants to get food to you faster, delivering it exactly when and where you want it. Not just those pizzas, but everything from meat and cheese to wine and coffee beans. The idea of curated food delivery began decades ago. Ask a baby boomer about Harry & David, a fruit producer that has delivered fruit to customers since the 1920s, and they will recall boxes of impeccable pears that arrived every Christmas holiday. But these days, delivery trucks pile up in our driveway as they bring us our grocery orders via Instacart, pints of ice cream delivered by GrubHub or Favor, or dinner via Doordash. Freshporter, a startup in Ventura, California, focuses on the Last Mile delivery "vessel" that holds prepared foods at your door at a temperature that maintains food safety. Tied together with tracking and tracing technology, this company intends to build a digitized national delivery network for companies that deliver prepared food.

Hundreds of new food delivery options appeared in early 2000, and by 2015, eighty-eight were operating to deliver food we ordered online.[5] Investors clambered aboard with millions of dollars of funding only to disappear when the surge abated by 2017. Food delivery companies were confronting the complications of logistics and the risks of disappointing both the sender and the recipient of their deliveries. Restaurants sued delivery companies that failed to deliver on time and to preserve the quality of the food. The costs and risks were piling up, and investors backed off as these new companies began to fail. And that's where Amazon's floating DC and drone delivery strategies could come in handy—moving some of that traffic off the road and into the air (see chapter 4).

New Trackers

Imagine the difficulties of tracking and tracing our food through this emerging network of delivery approaches. Some foods travel through existing routes; others through routes devised by the food companies. Waffle House could be a delivery hub, with its twenty-four-hour availability and its connection with truckers who fill up with pancakes. UPS will deliver your curated cheese box to one of its nearest Access Points (places it delivers to regularly, like a nearby drycleaner) to wait until you stop by on your regular visit. Hopefully, you keep your shirts crisp and clean often enough not to jeopardize the quality of the Stilton awaiting your arrival. Still, will there be a seamless tracking system that can hop over and through these various distribution networks?

Tracking food inside a single company is easy compared to the hybrid systems. Aside from companies such as Instacart that service a range of food stores, individual grocery stores are starting their own delivery services. Randalls, a grocery chain in Texas now owned by Safeway, began a grocery delivery service using its own fleet of trucks, while other grocery stores partner with logistics companies such as the Alabama-based Shipt or Texas-based Uship and Favor. These are logistics companies that deliver groceries but are also open to delivering just about anything.

The big food companies and grocery chains such as Walmart, Costco, Sam's Club, and Target are all working on new formats for food routes. In 2018, Kroger, arguably the largest grocery company in the world in terms of revenue, entered a partnership with Ocado, a UK online grocery company that will provide Kroger with logistics and warehousing expertise. Partnerships such as these are bound to continue as grocery and food service companies acquire and invest in logistics infrastructures in order to remain competitive in the e-commerce food industry.

With the continuing growth of online ordering of food and the demand for faster, fresher food delivery, these giants are working on trials and tests of anything from small-format delivery hubs to drive-through pickups for customers who order online to cooled boxes for in-store pickups. Just how a continuous tracking system will work while maintaining the choices demanded by today's consumers remains to be seen. Blockchain wants to be the unifying method, but as we will see later in this chapter, it's only in its infancy and will require more collaboration, standardization, and data sharing than many companies will tolerate.

Then there's Amazon and Google, both hard at work on delivery options that will roll out in the next few years. Ranging from AVs to distribution networks, these ambitious companies will be moving food closer and closer to us, most likely with minimal assistance from humans. Even though delivery services will bring more and more food directly to our kitchens, we will always have the option to go to physical grocery stores—they will just look a little different. (See chapter 6 for a peek.)

Now they are testing some pretty unusual solutions. While we demand trust in our food companies, Amazon and Walmart want us to deliver trust to them. In late 2017, Walmart announced its in-fridge delivery service.[6] Using a smart lock, we can now order groceries online from Walmart, and a delivery carrier will arrive at our house, let himself in, and place our purchases in our fridges, all while we watch remotely on the app.

Amazon and Alexa are also letting themselves into our homes. Through Amazon's Key, also announced in late 2017, Alexa invited us to let her deliver the food we'd ordered by sending Amazon's humans into our kitchens. And in early 2018, Amazon paid billions to acquire a smart doorbell company, RING, stepping up its commitment to entering your house. There's so much going on here: privacy, sharing, the Cloud, smart homes with smart kitchens, IoT. Alexa is already sitting on our shelf waiting for more things to do to justify its (her?) existence in our most intimate spaces. And soon, she may know what we want for dinner tonight and just go ahead have it delivered, at our regular meal time. In 2018, Amazon announced a service that delivers packages directly to your car. It's not clear if this will work for perishable food that requires cool temperatures. What's the limit to our willingness to allow strangers access to our homes and cars in return for convenience? Or maybe sending your packages to your car will keep your home off limits, retaining a private sanctuary for the newly open sourced world.

The consequences of this mash-up of technologies operating within our most private spaces are unimaginable right now. While many of us are intrigued, others are wondering how long we'll allow our personal boundaries to remain intact. But the lure of time savings, greater opportunities to enjoy the freedom of doing what we want when we want without hanging around the house waiting for a delivery . . . these are high-value ideas at the moment. But once we've let these services into our lives, not to mention kitchens, where will we find private spaces where we can be unguarded, unanalyzed, and unoptimized? Can we shut these technologies out once we've let them in? Will we want to? And why do some people resist the idea of someone entering their home, as if they have some remaining privacy after they've been living on Facebook and Google for years?

The Last Mile delivery of our food, including all these distribution options, is all part of the tracking and tracing conundrum. We've been pretty clear about the increasing demand for trust and transparency in our food system, and we know how trust plays into a solution. Inviting strangers into our kitchens and tracking their movements could be a daring move on our part. And tracking and tracing truck drivers is only part of the collision between personal privacy and the need to know everything about the things in our lives.

High-Stakes Tracking

But what about truly daring moves to track the movement of food, like those made by food logistics organizations and companies during natural disasters or military conflicts? Our need for transparency can sometimes collide with our national security needs—not to mention the competitive advantage of food companies. Distributing our food throughout the United States or the European Union is one thing. Trying to get armies fed in the burnt-out landscape of Syria or Iraq is another. Technology, infrastructure, and adaptability step in to make all that possible. Tracking and tracing food throughout a natural disaster is the ultimate stress test for food logistics managers. Knowing where those pallets of fresh water are every moment in their journey to a disaster relief site or refugee camp is a matter, truly, of life and death. Maria and Joe Riggio's pizza parlor's recovery after Hurricane Sandy in 2012 is an example of how food supply chains can navigate through weather crises

But while distorted and broken landscapes make food distribution tough, what about navigating combat zones to feed troops in the deserts of Iraq? US Colonel Chris Burke was tasked with feeding mobilized troops under attack with a food logistics system that was at risk of being blown up every day. As the head of logistics for the US Air Force in Iraq, Burke had been feeding US troops with the assistance of a logistics contractor. For twenty-five years, he had been in the thick of logistics planning as he exploited the adaptable nature of supply chains. During the 1990s, he provided logistics support for NATO's Operation Joint Guard. Hunkered down in the Balkans, Burke had juggled the food logistics needs of six European countries, each with its own food preferences. Eight military sites needed food and supplies for an international, transitional community. He remembered the difficulties of getting food across bombed out roads and over mountain passes mined by Serbian rebels, and how difficult it was to meet the prerequisites of the UN and NATO. But in 2010, while preparing for the transition to Operation Iraqi Freedom, he was worried. Colonel Burke supported a military strategy engaged in a withdrawal of troops after seven years of combat.[7] Burke led the logistics operations for the US Air Force during Operations Iraqi Freedom and New Dawn from 2008 to 2010. So his cities (dining facilities) were not only on the move under extreme conditions but also required a constant adjustment of supply quantities—and all while his logistics partners changed due to allegations of fraud. And he needed to track every food item as both his position and his customers were on the move.

Burke delivered pasta sauce and oregano (and much more) to hungry soldiers, State Department employees, and security contractors. Since his cities came out of nowhere, rising out of the landscape where no city had existed before, he had to build the food supply chain infrastructure from the ground up. He distributed the equipment needed to prepare the food and store the ingredients and the trucks and forklifts to move the food between ports and sites. He provided fuel to run the trucks, repair them, and tow them off sandy roads in the desert. Even more impressive was his plan for distribution of water in a country of deserts.

Food for the US military had to be brought in from outside Iraq. Every month, Burke's food logistics team delivered 2,400 truckloads of refrigerated food and 6.4 million pounds of fresh fruit and vegetables for meals eaten in 67 dining facilities (43 of which were mobile) set up in 10 staging areas, feeding 190,000 people every day. Burke was confronted with moving people, cities (dining facilities), and food in a landscape that required ingenious adaptation. His food supply chain pushed adaptability, reliability, trust, and technology to their extreme limits.

Most of the fresh fruit and vegetables—the most perishable and fragile of food items Burke ordered—came from Kuwait. The rest—dry goods and canned food—came from the United States in containers on cargo ships that left Port Elizabeth, New Jersey. This transit took about a month and moved truckloads of Quaker Oats and other American food through the Straits of Gibraltar and the Suez Canal to the ports in Kuwait. No wonder the troops in Iraq didn't get apples from Washington State.

Most cities gain and lose populations, but not as fast or as precipitously as Burke's cities. Burke had to address the transition of the US troops out of Iraq. Almost 160,000 troops were in Iraq in 2009 when President Obama announced a troop drawdown that would leave 42,000 in 2010. Burke had to figure out how to predict the amount of food to order while US troops were departing. Even in a city outside a conflict zone, food procurement personnel would be hard pressed to plan for such a rapid exodus of customers from all its dining facilities. Especially if food waste was a concern. How did Burke deal with this? He kept his eye on the supply chain and the troop withdrawal timeline at the same time. While stable cities increasingly adopt food-tracking software for the purpose of food safety, Burke added security as a top priority. For Iraq, the food supply chain traveled through hostile zones, areas where oversight is porous and problematic, to say the least. Docks teemed with workers who found a new container of pasta sauce an auspicious revenue source for their black market compatriots. The US military sites existed at the end of precarious and often damaged supply lines on roads that were open to attacks and disruption. Transparent food supply chains along these paths could bring devastating news, exploiting transparency for the illegal or terrorist activities.

As Burke's experience illustrates, food traceability and tracking makes it possible to make sure food gets to soldiers and civilians while minimizing loss and waste, both of food and humans. Whether food distributors move through the confused and broken landscapes of battlefields or just suffer traffic delays in congested cities, the design of our food distribution system contends with these roadblocks and still manages to function most of the time. But what happens when the distribution system goes dark, underground, and illegal? Billions of dollars of our food goes missing, is adulterated, or is simply stolen out of warehouses. This breakdown of food routes is a big reason that tracking and tracing food is so important and why investments in technology are offset by the recuperation of tons of food illicitly traded every day. Food tracking and tracing is a question of national security.

In Iraq, food supply lines could be hijacked, bombed, or sabotaged. While the need for trust is one reason to track and trace our food supply, the examples of combat zones and natural disasters point to extreme cases that require knowing where food is throughout the zone. (The issues around food safety discussed in chapter 3 also show how important it is to know where our food is.) If you don't know where the food has been, you can't track down supply chain failures or extract the contaminated food out of the supply chain.

In Iraq, Burke relied on his logistics food tracing and tracking service called the "Track and Trace System," a web-based program that enables clients to track their shipments in real time, watching as the container of pasta sauce leaves New Jersey or the truck convoy travels from Kuwait to Basra. While this sounded good to Burke, he sent an extra tractor and a tow truck along with his food-laden convoys and swathed his team with military security so the food traveled safely. This is when transparency can put your food supply and the entire army at risk. In case his convoys met up with a landmine or missile attack, a tractor could pull some loads out alongside a tow truck. During Burke's term in Iraq, he saw 33 fatalities, 262 casualties, 247 vehicle losses, 327 cargo losses, and two MIAs. These statistics reveal just how vulnerable food supply chains are when cities are in harm's way.

A US disaster relief agency, the Federal Emergency Management Agency (FEMA), emerged from relative obscurity following the 2001 attacks on the World Trade Center, and especially during Hurricane Katrina in 2005. Created by President Jimmy Carter in 1979, FEMA acts as the central food logistics coordinator when natural disasters occur in the United States. After the World Trade Center attack, FEMA became part of the new Department of Homeland Security. Like any other large government agency, the system is often encumbered by its own bureaucracy. For example, FEMA distribution coordinators lock up food donations organized by well-meaning citizens. During Hurricane Sandy in 2012, donated food (including twelve truckloads of bottled water donated by Nestlé) sat in community drop-off sites such as libraries while FEMA struggled to find a way to get it to people in Manhattan.[8] More bureaucratic red tape slowed down donations during Hurricane Sandy because New York's bottle law required all companies donating water to be certified as water distributors. So Anheuser-Busch's attempt to donate water was temporarily thwarted because it was only certified to distribute beer. Governor Cuomo eventually suspended these regulations, enabling water to reach thirsty survivors.[9] But still, in spite of the agency's claims that it had anticipated the city's emergency food and water needs, supplies were locked up in warehouses in Georgia even three days after the hurricane passed through New York. Then there was hurricane Maria in 2017, which caused Puerto Rico to lose its food supply chain for months. One reason was the US Jones Act that required the use of American-made ships with American crews to deliver cargo between US ports. There simply weren't enough of those ships to get food to Puerto Rico fast enough. President Trump temporarily waived the act so that food and other cargo could reach the distraught island, but the Jones Act remains in place, protecting the US shipping industry and harming the distribution of food supplies after disasters. The weight of federal and state administrations often combine with the effects of broken supply chains to create a food logistics system that creates its own disasters.

Mitigating these bureaucratic blockages, many private companies pitch in to supply cities in crisis. During the aftermath of Hurricane Katrina in 2005, Walmart sent truckloads of food to the Gulf Coast, utilizing its logistics network of vehicles, warehouses, and technology to feed survivors that FEMA failed to reach. Able to use plans already developed for crises that would impact business operations, private companies can scale existing response plans and protect assets while delivering food at the same time. Walmart's distribution center in Brookhaven, Mississippi, could fill trucks with supplies even before Katrina landed on the coast, and truckloads of water arrived before FEMA could get resources mobilized. Since FEMA can only set plans in motion, it often stumbles when organizations on the ground fail to implement plans or stumble around regulations or a lack of ready resources. During disasters, food supply chains operate with a situational combination of private and public services.

For natural disasters in the United States, Sysco partners with the Red Cross to plan food distribution through the Red Cross network. The company sends its mobile kitchens into disaster areas, as it did during Hurricane Katrina. Sysco's Disaster Plan, issued to its Eastern Maryland Region, outlines what to do when the US Weather Service declares a hurricane watch. The plan contains instructions for ordering extra supplies, but cautions that

Sysco won't make any promises about delivering any food in the forty-eight hours before a hurricane reaches landfall.[10] Other collaborations include coordination of international food aid organizations, such as the World Food Programme (WPF) and the American Logistics Aid Network (ALAN).[11] Joint exercises among ALAN, WPF, and other food aid organizations use simulations to get faster and lighter. These partnerships will improve as predictive software becomes more sophisticated and grounded in real-time analytics. The evolution of centralized distribution centers into a landscape of networked microwarehouses will also make feeding disaster areas more adaptive and less wasteful.

These emergency plans sometimes include a strategy called "leaning in," which increases delivery speed while lowering negative impacts upon the environment, but no amount of leaning can compensate for customers who want to lean in, themselves, by hoarding supplies at home. When I was living in Boston in 2010, a ruptured pipe connecting the water supply to the city precipitated a run on bottled water, causing stores to run out. Water, though not always considered food by many of us, is an essential ingredient for the preparation of food. In Boston that spring, some cafes and restaurants couldn't sell food because they had no water, and stores had not anticipated the impact of a multi-day water crisis. It's in these unpredictable situations that the adaptable nature of food supply chains breaks down. Risk-taking software and hindsight both have their limits. Before Hurricane Katrina, FEMA began stockpiling meals in the predicted path of the storm, in anticipation of a surge in demand. A system of tracking and tracing food in the supply chain along with predictive analytics could improve the provision of food to areas that experience these natural disasters.

But despite all good intentions, humanitarian food aid organizations around the world struggle to deliver to these sites. Leakage throughout the system, mishandling of food, lack of security, and spoilage continue. Corruption, bureaucracy, and byzantine regulations have made food aid almost its own worst enemy. Evidently, competing interests either block or spur developments that would improve transparency within our food system.

Pirates and Fraudsters

Food disappears from the global food supply chain every day. These leaks include piracy, theft, black markets, and adulteration of food products.

Piracy had existed as long as ships had carried valuable cargo, and it didn't end with the Barbary Pirates. Modern pirates operating off the coast of Somalia threatened shipping lanes and stalled cargo between 2008 and 2012. Although the number of piracy attacks began to decrease in 2010, they continue to cause dangerous friction in the supply chain. Walnuts, olive oil, honey, and other high value food falls into the hands of thieves all across the globe. Sometimes these ingredients are just stolen and sold on the black market; in other cases, they are adulterated and sold as the real thing. Improvements in tracking and tracing our food can help limit the amount of food diverted from our plates. On the other hand, too much transparency, or insecure systems for tracking food, will only enable offenders to be one step ahead of the law.

Food fraud, piracy, smuggling, adulteration, and other illicit activities impact the global food supply chain by siphoning off billions of dollars of food. Though, as we'll see later in the chapter, while compromises to our food system are often accidental, not all food contamination is. The adulteration of food was common in history as enterprising companies attempted to cheat customers by adding contaminants to extend quantities or enhance appearances. Adding chalk to milk in Victorian England is just one example. Adding rice syrup to honey in China is another, more contemporary example. Opportunities for sophisticated tracking and tracing technology abound in this environment.

In March 2016, Europol (the European Union's law enforcement agency), in cooperation with Interpol, announced a historic seizure of "fake" food, also called "adulterated" or "fraudulent" food. The two organizations seized more than ten thousand tons of fraudulent food and a million liters of fraudulent drink from fifty-seven countries.[12] In 2012, US Customs officials discovered counterfeit ketchup in a New Jersey warehouse. The counterfeiters bought regular Heinz ketchup and repacked it in bottles with labels for the premium Heinz ketchup hoping to benefit from the price difference between the regular and higher-priced condiments.

By now, food safety laws and testing methods can usually detect when our milk contains chalk. But like doping in the sports world, as the methods for detecting contaminants have become available, the adulterers have found other contaminants that escape the testing methods. Transparency only allows the signaling of preventative measures so that offenders can develop workarounds.

Food fraud today continues to grow, both because the organizations conducting illegal food trade are more sophisticated and because the value and amount of international food trade has increased. The March 2016 heist included nine tons of fertilizer-contaminated sugar found in Egypt. Other captured food included monkey meat, caterpillars, and fake whisky and wine, along with items unfit for human consumption and banned for use in food.

In December 2015, the Italian police found seven thousand tons of fake olive oil.[13] Fraud and contamination of olive oils has increasingly been a problem since the Mediterranean Diet became popular. Legitimate manufacturers needed a way to verify that their oil was the real thing, so in Tuscany, Italy, oil producers began to use NFC RFID sensors embedded in the bottle labels.

Olive oil isn't the only target of fraud by insiders trying to save a buck, or outsiders trying to make one. In 2013, British newspapers horrified beef-loving readers with the news that Irish horsemeat had found its way into the beef supply chain late in 2012. Meat inspectors discovered the horsemeat in frozen hamburgers that supplied supermarkets such as Tesco and Aldi. Using DNA samples, food inspectors were able to track the horsemeat back through the supply chain to food processing companies in France that made food products such as lasagna using the mislabeled meat. Tracking the meat revealed just how complex the food supply chain can be. Some of it was slaughtered in Romania and then sold through several food traders in the Netherlands and Cyprus before ever reaching the French food manufacturers.[14] The UK investigated the National Food Crime Unit and the Food Crime Intelligence Network among a collection of response and protection measures.

The US Food Protection and Defense Institute (FPDI), part of the Homeland Security Center of Excellence, has a charming term for food fraud: Economically Motivated Adulteration (EMA).[15] The Institute offers the food industry a virtual tool for simulating instances of food fraud to determine the most effective defense tactics.

According to FPDI, about 7 percent of the food commerce in the United States contains fraudulent ingredients.[16] It uses web-based tools to monitor and track food safety throughout the United States by assessing risks, cyber security, traceability, detection tools, and response methods. In 2015, the US Pharmacopeial Convention (USP), an international group of members that monitors the integrity of food and drugs, declared illegal food traffic was growing at an annual rate of 60 percent, and with the growing complexity and volume of food sent through the global food supply chain, the opportunities for food fraud only increase.[17] And it means big bucks for those who succeed in sending adulterated or fake food through our global food supply chain.

Sometimes illegal supply chains develop to avoid trade sanctions, antidumping regulations, or laws against certain drugs or ingredients, such as some antibiotics. These issues played into the illegal shipments of Chinese honey in 2014, when a Chinese businessman living in Texas smuggled several tons of honey through Houston.[18] It wasn't the first time China had been caught committing food fraud. In 2008, contaminated powdered milk produced in China caused the death of six babies. Inadequate and poorly administered food safety laws have created mistrust of Chinese food, and even now the repercussions are still felt in the global powdered milk supply chain. Foreign companies stepped in to supply the Chinese market, and many are still the main suppliers to China. While not exactly food fraud, the milk scandal exemplifies dishonest representation of food quality, which in most countries is unlawful.[19] And it impacts other producers in the global food supply chain. When milk adulteration appeared in China, China bought more milk from the United States and Australia, driving up demand for dairy exports in both those countries.

Most of us are unaware that we may be eating flounder instead of halibut, but the seafood supply chain has made progress identifying and tracking food. Oceana, a nonprofit organization founded in 2011 to protect the world's oceans, conducted several studies about mislabeling seafood. In its 2013–2014 report about salmon, Oceana revealed that 43 percent of the salmon sold around the world was mislabeled.[20] In most cases, salmon was labeled as wild rather than farmed. And a 2012 study by researchers at UCLA and Loyola Marymount University found that 47 percent of the sushi in twenty-six sushi restaurants in Los Angeles was mislabeled.[21] While some of these mistakes could be simply mistakes, some are intentional due to significant cost differences between fish species. In 2016, the National Oceanic and Atmospheric Administration (NOAA) issued regulations to try to track down and eliminate mislabeling of imported seafood.

Needless to say, illegal food shipments through hidden supply chains are big business. This means tracking and tracing food has become even more complicated as a result of the need for product verification. Both the organic and non-GMO supply chains require trackable, verifiable data to certify that foods are what they say they are. Food safety inspectors aren't on the front line for these illicit dealings—the FBI, CIA, and international intelligence agencies such as Interpol are on the job.

Clear Labs, a startup founded in 2013 and located in Silicon Valley, uses DNA profiling to detect fraudulent seafood identification.[22] Cofounder Mahni Gorashi and his team use next-gen DNA testing along with a database food index to analyze food in the supply chain. Its product can determine the identity of food ingredients at the molecular level, which is critical from an economic point of view, but also from a public health perspective. Detecting gluten or other allergens could help mitigate risk for food products. Other scientists and startups are exploring this area with innovations that will make DNA identification of our food less costly and more timely.

The concern about food fraud crosses over into concerns about food safety, since any food that is not accurately identified and in conformance with safety standards could contain toxins or other ingredients harmful to human health. In the case of the British horsemeat incident, sometimes referred to as "Horsegate," the government was especially keen to reestablish public trust in the food system. The report pointed out that the difficulties around financial sustainability motivate small food businesses to cut corners, sometimes using below-standard ingredients or illegal, lower-cost suppliers.[23] The investigation also pointed out that more complicated supply chains are more prone to fraud, since tracking illegal ingredients through complicated paths is often nearly impossible. The potential for preventing food fraud is one argument for local food production that requires fewer intermediate steps before reaching consumers. This may make sense except for the fact that a single producer could arguably be the source for adulteration.

Even the legal food supply chain has its own challenges for tracking and tracing nonconforming food. Coexistence of food production systems for organic, non-GMO ingredients creates an even more urgent requirement for supply chain monitoring, tracking, and tracing. Producers need to certify that their foods are what they say they are on labels and in marketing campaigns, as cross-contamination risks legal action and penalties by enforcement bodies. Several systems help food suppliers comply with these safety regulations and standards. One such company, Safety Chain, manages vendors. When the lettuce supplier sells its lettuce to Wendy's, Wendy's uses a software platform like Safety Chain to crosscheck lettuce quality with produce safety standards and log compliance. These systems check to see whether food meets safety and quality standards set both by the government and private industry. Wendy's also wants to know that those burgers are all the right size for its buns.

Smarter Trackers

Security issues aside, tracking and tracing is critical to the actual sourcing of food products. Upscale restaurants strive to find the latest, freshest ingredients for an ever-more sophisticated consumer, but finding those costly ingredients and making sure they arrive fresh requires the latest tracking technology. In 2009, *Wired Magazine* ran a story about Chef Paul Bartolotta, who ran a Ristorante di Mare in Las Vegas until 2015.[24] He was known for his ability to get fresh seafood from the Mediterranean to Las Vegas, "pier to platter," in less than 48 hours. Fishermen and buyers in Italy used Skype to show Bartolotta prospective catches, and after Bartolotta decided to purchase fish out of one of those catches, the buyer made sure one fish in each container carried a microchip. On the next flight out of Milan, the chips recorded internal temperatures every twenty minutes throughout the journey to Las Vegas. These tracking sensors are also found in more containers, tracking temperatures and other events. Tracking information is seen by today's consumers as value added to their food products. They are willing to pay more for a detailed description of their meal from farm to plate. This trend will continue until the information becomes standard fare for all our food. Recent research indicates that tracking information is valued more than speed when it comes to delivering food. A consumer would rather wait an extra hour or day if it means food arrived with a more complete record of its travels.

Consider Glanbia, a small nutritional food company in Ireland.[25] Many of its products use milk collected from Irish dairies, and it optimizes its truck fleet with sensors at strategic points along its supply chain. The sensors on the trucks gather data about both the quantity and quality of the milk they transport. The quality of the milk determines where the truck will deliver its shipment. For example, if the milk contains more cream, the truck will deliver the cream-laden milk to Glanbia's cream processing facility.[26] If the milk sensor determines a load has less cream than is desirable for cream production, the data will instruct the driver to go to the facility that removes whey from the milk to produce nutritional supplements. GEA Food Solutions, a large food processing equipment manufacturer in the Netherlands, makes the sensors Glanbia uses to gather the milk data.[27]

Driscoll's, a multi-billion-dollar berry company located in California, uses RFID chips to monitor berry shipments in real time. Perishable fruit is delicate, so devices such as those made by Sendum track "shock events" and vibrations.[28] Each bump and vibration can break down the fruit, causing significant loss of shelf life. Studies of shipments from Thailand explain how these vibration sensors, used in both rail and truck transport, provide valuable data that shippers can use to improve their produce logistics.[29] If they find that trucks incur intense vibration at the rear of the trailer, shippers can locate the problems and determine the necessary repairs.

Driscoll's is making progress toward the integration of multiple technologies to enhance its tracking system, including artificial intelligence and machine learning. We see plastic containers of berries in stores around the world that are distributed through Driscoll's facilities in California and Florida. (When the seasons change, Driscoll's can grow the berries in climate-compatible fields somewhere in the world so that consumers can buy berries at any time of the year—another example of how adaptability and reliability keep the supply chain moving.)

All the data that Driscoll's accumulates goes into a Data Lake, a database with a flat architecture (not hierarchical like most of the databases we commoners use) that stores raw data. To enhance berry tracking, it uses the Lake to contain data collected from its trucks that use geolocation software. Companies such as Driscoll's use the tracking technology to certify the integrity of supply chains not only for GMO foods but also for fair trade and organic validation.

Other food companies are moving toward smarter packaging that enables more detailed tracking and tracing of the movements of products throughout the supply chain. Avery Dennison developed a sensor for the pharmaceutical industry that goes on the inside or outside of a package. In the case of Desert Farms, a California company that ships camels' milk for Amish producers, the sensors go both inside and out, logging the temperature of the milk and the environment.[30] Labels, sensors, scanners, and other technologies are all coming together to make our food's routes knowable and transparent.

Fourkites has a real-time temperature tracker that tracks the interior temperatures of shipping containers and other cargo containers. Companies such as Smithfield Meat can track and certify temperatures in real time so they can be more responsive should there be any food safety related incidents. Trackers have other advantages, too. Recipients of food deliveries often have time periods during which their loading docks are open, warehouse space is available, and staff is on hand to receive shipments. These scheduling windows offer a shipper the opportunity to deliver during times when they can avoid waits at the loading dock. With a tracker that can project an estimated time of arrival (ETA), both the shipper and the receiver can synchronize deliveries within the best timeframe. Much like ride-sharing apps these days, this projected ETA, when perfected, could do much to limit the time reefer trucks hang out around the corner waiting for a spot at the loading dock.

Whether for our own need for trust, optimization of the supply chain, or for the purpose of locating adulterated or unsafe food, tracing food back through the supply chain makes it possible to recall food to ensure that public health isn't threatened and to identify where the supply chain broke down. Technology for recalls has come a long way. When London experienced a series of cholera outbreaks during the 1800s, the first response was to blame the fetid city air, until a physician named John Snow located a contaminated water pump. Back then, it was difficult to detect fraud or contamination in food—and nearly impossible to remove the compromised ingredients from the supply chain. The science of food testing and the technology for detecting contamination was not available until the twentieth century.

Backtracking Food

Food safety becomes even more challenging and critical under crisis conditions because time is of the essence when death is in the pot. Just ask Chipotle or Blue Bell Ice Cream about food tracking, and we'll hear about the stressful moments spent finding and recalling contaminated products. When Blue Bell Ice Cream got word that the ice cream in one of their

Oklahoma facilities was contaminated with listeria, the company went "one-up-one-back," meaning they investigated suppliers of ice cream ingredients one step before they arrived at the ice cream plant and one step after.[31] This approach provides a systematic way for companies to search through their supply chains for the source of an outbreak or contamination. In Blue Bell's case, they found evidence of possible contamination at the plant that provided cookie dough for their cookie dough ice cream. This contamination was not inconsequential; three people died as a result of eating the adulterated ice cream. These events do more to erode the trust consumers have for food and food companies and, as we've noted, it's that trustworthiness that underlies the smooth operation of the food supply chain. Trust is fragile, to say the least.

In Chipotle's case, seventeen restaurants in eight states reported that customers were hospitalized with Shiga toxin-producing *E. coli* infections. No one food ingredient was found to have caused the outbreak, which goes to show how much more complicated food safety is for companies that use a large number of suppliers and ingredients for a single dish. Like other restaurants, many of Chipotle's menu items include multiple ingredients that are combined in a single serving, so tracking down the reason your burrito made you sick isn't such an easy task.

The Center for Disease Control (CDC) described the process for tracking down the problem, including a new technique that uses DNA to fingerprint the *E. coli* in the victims, enabling investigators to trace the contaminant throughout Chipotle's system.[32] PulseNet, a global network of labs, tells the CDC where a particular strain of *E. coli* may travel, enabling it to relate a source of contamination to a group of individuals.[33] The CDC says that the network tracks about 280 clusters of food-borne illnesses, areas of a high incidence of a disease outbreak, every year.[34]

Whole Genome Sequencing (WGS) is also a tool for identifying the exact strain drifting through the food system. We'll see more and more digital identification technology in our food supply chain applied for just this purpose, identifying the molecular nature of food as it travels within the supply chain. Facial recognition technology will also make identification and validation of perishable food and ingredients possible as they move through the supply chain. Robots and scanners that use facial recognition, blockchain, and sensors will virtually replace human inspectors and instead rely on artificial intelligence and Big Data.

Not only will the ingredients be checked for safety and integrity, the ethical labor practices of a food supplier can be certified through digital verification of compliance with ethical sourcing standards for the food supply chain. This goes beyond just verifying the additives supplied during the processing stage and the information provided on food labels. This level of verification goes to the heart of consumers' trust issues when it comes to "big food."

What happens to all that food when it is recalled due to noncompliance or a breakout of a food-borne illness? Before the Food Safety Modernization Act (FSMA), food recalls were voluntary, but now the US government requires them. Some of the recalled food goes into landfills, some goes into animal food, and some can be cooked and repurposed. Yes, you read that right. The contaminated food can go right back into the chain for human consumption, though the FDA does require that it be pasteurized or cooked first.[35] It's also not clear whether all of the recalled products are recovered. What happens to the rest?

The USDA's Food Safety and Inspection Service (FSIS) states that companies can cook the recovered food, such as meat, to create a secondary supply that could be combined with other ingredients and sold to the public. This practice isn't illegal—it's what the US regulations allow. Other countries, both developed and underdeveloped, have their own standards, and while many are less stringent in some ways than the EU or US standards, they are continually improving food safety practices in order to meet requirements for export to the developed countries.[36]

Recalls occur outside the United States as well, since food-borne illnesses are a problem worldwide. The European Commission has a Rapid Alert System for Food and Feed (RASFF), established in 1979, that provides all members quick access to alerts, notifications, and disposal status regarding unsafe food within the European Union.[37] In 2015, Japan caught contaminated Gorgonzola cheese imported from Italy and reported it to RASFF so other countries that may have received the cheese could be notified.

To mitigate the risk of contamination and recall as food moves across borders in the United States, APHIS handles safety and security by ruling the international movement of food.[38] If the supply chain moves food across state or national boundaries, APHIS dictates how it's done. If a shipper sends oranges from Seville, Spain, that shipper must comply with specific APHIS regulations. Those oranges may be denied entry if APHIS has received information about boycotts or diseases and pests that affect them. Once a ship lands a container, APHIS inspectors can determine whether the shipment requires fumigation and direct a shipper to one of its approved services before the fruit can be stored in the United States.

Beyond just the cost of pulling products off the shelf, additional expenses accrue, such as creating a public relations campaign to offset the negative publicity and incurring revenue loss. A company may find its consumers aren't as forgiving as Blue Bell's fans. When Blue Bell recalled its ice cream in 2015, customers were concerned, but the real fans were anxious for the ice cream to reappear on the shelves. The empty locations on store shelves where their beloved ice cream had once lived were only a sad reminder that their favorite sweet treat would be on a hiatus until it sorted things out back at the factory. It did, in late 2015, and consumers rejoiced.

But in other cases, usually with larger companies, consumers aren't so patient and are demanding greater transparency. Brand contamination is a consequence of food contamination. The reputation of a company can, as in Chipotle's case, be held in question as outbreaks are investigated. Consider the contaminated spinach in 2006 from Earthbound Farm, with its reputation for healthy, organic produce. As it turned out, it wasn't the company's spinach exactly that was the culprit; it was an Angus beef rancher's contaminated field that caused the problem when Earthbound contracted with the rancher to grow spinach.[39] But still, the responsibility and reputational damage landed squarely on Earthbound's shoulders. And as a result of the public outcry over the use of what the media called "pink slime" to process meat, one meat processor sued a media outlet, ABC, for damages. The company, Beef Products, Inc. (BPI) in South Dakota, closed three of its four processing units as a result of the negative publicity; ABC and BPI settled the lawsuit in 2017.[40]

Food companies, processors, packaging companies, and distributors—and just about everyone in the food supply chain—take food safety more seriously than ever now that the slightest oversight can lead to litigation and brand besmirching. Brian Weale from the food service company Sysco relates how diligent his company is about tracking and reporting food safety problems. When a food safety issue is reported anywhere in the supply chain, the information travels throughout the chain that handles that item. Recorded phone calls go to anyone who received the product; if the buyer doesn't listen to the entire phone message, the recall system will continually redial the buyer until he or she has heard all the information related to the recall. No hang-ups, please.

Blockchain: The New Superpower?

Finding food in the supply chain for the purpose of recalls is about to become easier, thanks to the increased interest in blockchain technology. You may remember the Chinese company using blockchain to track its chickens. Thousands of years ago, the Chinese used other methods of tracking food shipments: written ledgers and imprints on clay amphorae, for example. By the 1700s, shippers accounted for cargo with ledgers for signing goods they handled in and out. Shipping companies gathered up the ledgers to track goods as they passed through many hands, down what we call the "chain of custody," which ensured each handler was held accountable for the condition of the goods during the period they were in his possession. Similar to the bills of lading for ships, a ledger for tracking food-related shipments entailed a simple note that logged the time in and the time out of the facilities of anyone that handled a shipment. Today the ledger can take the form of a blockchain, a database that contains a time-stamped log of each transaction as it moves between peers, in real time.

The reason blockchains are of interest in the food supply chain is the claim that the database is secure. Once an item passes through the hands of each peer on the network, the information about the shipment, including the timing of the transaction, cannot be easily altered. Complex algorithms store the information and the network remembers each transaction. A bushel of apples moving from the producer to your grocery store leaves a series of time-stamped data records that accumulate through the network, allowing anyone in the system to check on the status of a shipment independently.

Blockchains also solve the food industry's custody issue. When the blockchain digitally offers an item to a peer and the peer accepts the offer, an implied transference of property occurs throughout the network as that bushel of apples moves toward the customer. Instead of an apple producer selling apples to a grocery distributor through a bank transaction, the producer's financial transaction—actually delivering the title to the apples—happens directly with the distributor.

In essence, you have a distributed ledger, allowing transparency to all within the system. In reality, you have the old bill of lading in a digital form in a common ledger. The information contained in that one document exists in many computers in the network along the way. So every time a bushel of apples moves through its supply chain, information about its steps are recorded, including who moved it, when, why, and what resulted from the movement. The data form blocks that leave unique "fingerprints" along the chain. Any attempt to change that fingerprint travels throughout the entire chain, alerting everyone that the integrity of the chain was compromised. If someone steals an apple, the blockchain will know where and when it disappeared.

There are many applications for blockchain within the food system: fraud prevention, food safety, recall tracking, and identification of illegal food production such as the use of slave labor or environmentally unsustainable practices.[41] Food safety is the key driver, since successful tracking to identify and eliminate food contamination saves lives.

Research and development on blockchains for supply chains is underway in both the food industry and academia. In October 2016, three big players in the food supply chain announced a collaboration that will add to the momentum for the food supply chain to engage with blockchain technology. IBM with its Big Data and artificial intelligence centers, Tsinghua University (the Chinese center for development of blockchain technology), and Walmart with its deep knowledge of the grocery business are working to enable transparency through blockchain tracking on a global scale. Even before these big three came together, the Co-operative Group in the UK announced its blockchain-based program, Provenance, which creates a record of transactions as food moves from producers to its 3,500 stores in Britain.

Blockchains could revolutionize far more than just the movement of food. IBM has suggested that blockchains could record crop data, climate conditions, and the moisture content of food. This would allow warehouse operators to plan for storage requirements in advance of grain delivery, for example. Of course, all the new cloud-based technology and mobile applications make tracing and tracking more effective and, eventually, more cost-effective. But success with blockchain technology will depend upon the entire food supply chain industry to agree to standards that would create an industry platform. Who will control the platform and create the standards?

Not to herd more chickens into this chapter, but they seem to be everybody's use test case. In early 2018, a new brand developed in partnership with Future Market. Block Bird is a chicken product with an interactive e-ink package that communicates the entire life cycle of the specific chicken in a package. The combined technologies of smart packaging and blockchain make this possible. We can now buy a Block Bird and know how our bird was raised, what it ate, and how it was handled throughout its life before its moment of fricassee. This is possible only with the inclusion of sensors and management of Big Data all along the way, from the chicken yard to your kitchen. Replacing handwritten notes, incompatible databases, and divergent practices, this idea of a fully traceable supply chain is the hope of those who want transparent, trustworthy food. These products are only in their early stages, and they still have major barriers to overcome before we have a flock of products to choose from. But it seems the chickens are leading the way.

But wait. Are all these tracking and tracing technologies a good thing? While the technology gathers data about the things moving in the Internet of Food, it also captures data about us, the consumers. Sure, we want to know where our food comes from and how it gets to us, but that data drags us along with it. While following cargo throughout a supply chain isn't new, the transparency we're about to have will be. Innovations like temperature trackers and data loggers for food shipments have been around for decades, and they are getting cheaper and capable of operating on mobile devices. And some observers note that even a blockchain database could be hacked or data forged.

Despite the clear advantages of tracking and tracing technologies like these, they're not universally loved. Truck drivers, for example, have not been eager to embrace GPS trackers, also called electronic logging devices (ELDs) by the trucking industry, for their trucks. Both independent and unionized drivers argue that the use of such trackers is an invasion of privacy and too costly to implement. In June 2017, the Supreme Court refused to consider an appeal against the ruling that required the use of such trackers. But the argument may be moot; we may be watching the transition to driverless trucks as supply chain integration progresses.

Also resistant to these innovations are the many small farms that eschew the use of any technology that supplants the wisdom and experience of farmers. Farmers, particularly American farmers, come from a tradition of independence and frontier-based values. Although cooperatives have been commonplace, total integration and collaboration on a large scale isn't taken for granted. In Europe, where the distances are shorter and the economic and political philosophies are more cooperative, integration of data systems and agreement on practices is more easily digested.

And on a personal level, those tags we talked about don't just measure temperature and vibrations. All that data goes to the Cloud, where it hangs around until tapped by the company using the system. The data can do more than just track a strawberry's progress from the field to your shortcake. It can add points to your consumer loyalty program, signal inventory status, register products, and perhaps even send recipe information from the company's test kitchen to you, the consumer, who is now linked to the kitchen through the product sensor. So the digital label becomes the umbilical cord tying customers to producers and distributors. Once you pick up that apple and put it in your grocery cart, there's no telling what that label may be communicating to the apple marketing department.

One also wonders about the impact of all this transparency and data sharing upon the food industry. How will they manage innovation, research, and development for technologies that they consider intellectual property? Will they ever become unsiloed? Remember that researchers at academic institutions such as MIT want agricultural data to be in an open system, not proprietary to those companies that manufacture farm equipment. Will transparency limit the risks companies are willing to take along the road to improving the trust factor? In today's cultural climate of collaboration, equity, and inclusion, it will be increasingly difficult for food and agricultural companies to maintain a closed system and proprietary data standards. On the other hand, the more open our food system becomes and the more data collected within the supply system that is visible, the more vulnerable our global food system may be to hackers, adulterers, and anyone else who wants to stall or bypass our food supply chain.

Millennials and Gen Zers seem to be willing to trade privacy for transparency and convenience. But that could change as more and more people watch episodes of *Black Mirror* or find their bank accounts depleted. We haven't reached that point yet, but we're heading in the direction of open access to our genomes, buying habits, driving habits, and eating habits.

Soon enough, companies that sell us our food will use our personal health data to push food that our insurance companies and employers want us to eat. Restaurants will not only be able to tell you all about Colin the chicken, but also how Colin fits your particular taste preferences and health data. Maybe even your health data as of the moment you stepped into the restaurant. Are we giving up too much privacy in exchange for a transparent, trusted food system? Probably not, but be prepared for a push-back, because there always is one.

6 The Future: New Roots and Routes Ahead

Writing a book now, in 2018, about the future of the global food supply chain, sometimes feels fruitless. As we've seen, the ground is shifting every day: large food distributors are setting up their own startup incubators or investing in those already working on our new food supply chain. Startups are continuing to come up with ideas for tracking food, extending shelf life without artificial preservatives, and connecting local producers to regional markets. Our old institutions, such as the USDA and the Grocery Manufacturers Association (GMA) are finding it difficult to remain relevant in the current, fast-paced, improvisational business cycle. Big Food, Big Agriculture, Big Anything, is feeling the pressure to look small, transparent, and trustworthy. Fissures in the established health industry reveal the imminent breakup of manual record keeping, and institutions that are professional gatekeepers are showing signs of becoming marginalized. The ripple effects from these changes are seeping into the way we produce, prepare, and deliver food. By the time this book appears in a bookstore, its expiration date may have passed.

We recognize the emergence of a new food system. What was only a suggestive shape with vague contours in 2018 has by now become a system with a distinctly different topography that will change the way we feed cities around the world. Key components of the new food supply chain will include personalization, localization, and transparency. Convenience will endlessly spar with social values in any product or service within the new supply chain. The intersection of health care and our food system will cause one of those contests against the traditional knowledge of owners and individuals who will demand more control over their lives. Promises of access to our own health data and the means to manage our own bodies are emerging from below, not from above. The American healthcare system is still in the process of its own remaking.

The means for moving our food will exist within new networks, some distributed, some centralized. Vehicle manufacturers are announcing their commitment to electric, autonomous trucks and cars. Small, new companies are tracking, tracing, and optimizing our food shipments. Drones and robots are seeking and sometimes finding opportunities to make food deliveries in the Last Mile in cities all over the world. And standards-making, open-systems-oriented groups are making progress toward a shared and open system for food. These networks will transport more of our food as energy, in digital form rather than physical.

Technology continues to inhabit our food culture, and we are struggling to find a way to have our cake and eat it too, embracing automation while preserving the sensorial, social meaning of mealtime. We will continue to seek a balance, and we are only now discovering the complexities of reengineering our food system in this digital age. Will traditional dirt farms disappear? Probably not, but look for ways they will change, along with the new farmers who operate them.

In spite of the rapid-fire technological advancements that are changing every aspect of our daily lives, we still run into logjams that require us to handle things "the old-fashioned way." We continue to deal with paper jams in our office printers. Google Maps still directs us to dead-end roads. And Siri insists she can't understand us. And in many ways, our food system stalls as the established logistics system hangs on and innovations lag behind other industries. Most of our food system is still rooted in the traditional practices of soil-based agronomy and animal husbandry.

We're seeing this transformation while still encumbered by old technology and infrastructures, not to mention global political and economic instability and environmental uncertainties. Our global transportation infrastructure, for example, is stressed—literally and figuratively. Trains are slow to adopt GPS tracking systems. An Amtrak collision in early 2018 could have been avoided with existing GPS technology for "positive train control." Truckers who resist the electronic logging devices that track their movements reluctantly accept the trackers while finding ways to spoof the devices or just ignoring the law. Predictions are that, despite their potential safety benefits, the devices will lengthen delivery times and raise food prices.

While our old work cultures and systems linger, younger generations want meaning, action, transparency, and convenience. They have little patience for old, opaque institutions, and they thrive on collaboration and move toward the new sharing economy. Try to find a millennial or Generation Zer who is excited about the notion of having our food produced by one or three global companies that operate with little transparency.

The global structure of the food industry is changing. Car companies announce AVs for food delivery, grocery chains gobble up logistics companies, and AI and blockchain technology find new applications for tracking and tracing even the smallest crumb on the way to our plates.

As we seek the human-digital balance in our food system, we observe the acceleration of change with the hope that what lies just beyond the next few years is a new food system that rights all the wrongs we've learned of during the past decade: food waste, harmful additives, unfair labor practices, harm to our environment, famine, and obesity, for example.

Hang on to your forks, as we're about to receive reimagined food in unimagined ways. Imagine that.

Two Futures?

Although we can agree that the global food system is changing, our visions for its future vary widely. Some of us desire a leveling of Big Food, a redistribution of land and ownership that enables small farmers to remain on farms, and food that is fresh and free of industrial processing. The futures outlined here focus on how technology will impact the future of food, deferring social and political change for another discussion. Tech-driven changes that impact how we feed ourselves won't be easy to accept. They will challenge us to reconsider time-honored traditions of what it means to sit around a table and enjoy a good meal with friends. The changes ahead will also radically transform developing countries and underserved populations that have struggled to feed themselves for centuries. For the first time, we may see how technology can enable these groups to produce, access, and consume more food at lower costs . . . a long-term goal, but one that has up to now been elusive and frustrating.

What will future look like? While we can (and will) speculate based on what we know about today's food system and the developments in progress, all we know for certain is that we don't yet know for certain. While it may be exhilarating to envision a future that includes a twenty-first-century version of the Jetsons' Food-a-Rac-a-Cycle (a food-synthesizer), we may experience one of two futures: one evolutionary and the other revolutionary.

Food Systems 2.0 and 3.0

We need these two views of our future because it's unclear how successful technology will be in replacing humans while providing convenient, safe, and affordable food. After all, we know that we humans are wary of who makes, prepares, and delivers our food. And if the years ahead bring an economic crisis, an outbreak of food-borne illnesses due to terrorists, or cyberattacks on supply chain industry companies such as Maersk or DHL that halt efforts to be transparent and open, all these hypothetical events could significantly alter any path we may take today toward one future or another.

Or consider that instead of having the luxury of choosing between these future scenarios, we may discover that our choices will be made for us. The evolutionary model may continue until that tipping point arrives and the food system as we know it suddenly leaps into the revolutionary model. Imagine a time when there's just enough AI, IoT, machine learning, networks, and smart devices that they suddenly gang up on us and we find our plates are unrecognizable. This scenario isn't meant as a doomsday forecast but rather as a reminder that change doesn't always follow tidy timetables.

Remember the pizza from Pizza Suprema in New York in 2018? That shop will look and act differently in our two imagined futures. Since we're allowing for two futures, one that is more dramatically different from today's food system than the other, we can take two runs at imagining Joe's world in the future, allowing for two scenarios for the role of technology in our food system.

The first future, the evolutionary future, applies technology in more distributed networks to the friction points in our existing food supply chain. The technologies will be familiar to us, and we will already be adapting to their use in our existing food system. "Paper jams" will persist, causing friction in the movement to a new system. Some technological solutions may backfire, causing consumers to reconsider how much of their cultural connection with food they are willing to trade in for convenience. Of course, those who do not want to give up control of data will cause a lag in the adoption of these new systems. And some of us will persist with the belief that we shouldn't hand off our food system to engineers and their new technologies. Those who resisted genetically modified organisms will find it difficult to embrace lab meat.

The second, revolutionary future, breaks from the past and delivers an entirely new food supply chain enabled by technology and designed by engineers. Our food system will include new tools that will appear to some of us as modern, highly intelligent variations of the 1960s Food-a-Rac-a-Cycle. Some of the technologies used in this future are today only discussed in labs and with a combination of nervous anticipation and wide-eyed wonderment. The Singularity of Food may have arrived.

In this second future, we've overlooked "paper jams" in much the same way as we have throughout the decades since digital printers arrived. In this future, few traditional farmers remain, and those who do have IT staffs. The food system consists of tech companies that use their digital tools to produce food, among other things. Expectations for farming have changed from subsidized businesses and nonprofit endeavors to financially sustainable, scalable enterprises. Many food companies have social values woven into their DNA and thrive within a shared economy.

Today, the food industry is struggling to make sense of new technologies, climate changes, and uncertain economic times. It is responding to consumer demands for healthier food at lower costs for more people. Big Food is worried and is pulling in startups in order to keep its own brands relevant. Some are setting up their own internal incubators, such as Chobani and Campbell's Soup Company. Others are partnering with tech incubators and developing their own venture funds, such as Tyson Ventures. Startups are challenging the idea of being "Big" in the first place. The traditional competitive advantage of expensive, big supply chain networks may not apply in an era when startups can appear from nowhere and deliver fresh food directly to our plates.

Cities will become more involved, along with their humans, in the design of urban food systems. Silos will be emptying out as technology networks knowledge across business sectors. In our twenty-first-century business culture, a meditation app partners with a food supplement service that partners with a personalized nutrition app that partners with a network of healthcare services that partners with a network of urban farms. Change is happening from below, not from the sole survivors at the top—unless, of course, they have the smarts to integrate innovation from outside.

Let's rattle our assumptions, hopes, and wishes for our future food system and expand our imagination.

The Evolutionary Future: Food 2.0

In 2018, we were being fed news about vertical farms, 3-D printed food, and blockchain technology. These developments were tantalizing teasers suggesting something new was about to arrive, but they were not quite ambitious enough to connect all the activities in our food system. Each idea had its own promise, but hardly anyone could think about how all these bits and bytes would fit together. And the food industry was slow in standardizing and sharing data needed to create an open network for the food supply chain. Some companies outright refused, frightened by incidences of cyberattacks and the specter of losing brand leadership based on sourcing expertise.

What We Eat

In this imagined future, Joe still uses foodservice companies such as Sysco, but Sysco now looks more like Cisco. Sysco bought a group of startups and began investing in technologies that enabled them to distribute food faster and at a lower cost while preserving freshness throughout its distribution system. About half of Joe's produce comes from a nearby urban farm located in a group of shipping containers. But the urban farm can't provide sufficient quantities with enough variety to fulfill all of Joe's needs, and the container-grown food is more expensive since it specializes in small-lot production. Deliveries from the containers arrive on autonomous shuttles that specialize in Last Mile delivery routes.

Joe's inventory system looks different now, too. He can keep more fresh food in stock now, since scientists have found more natural solutions for extending shelf life. And keeping plenty of fresh produce on hand is necessary now that half of Joe's customers are vegetarians or vegans. Much of the land formerly used for livestock production has been converted to vegetable protein production to meet demand and lower food prices.

Joe has more options for pizza toppings, including some engineered, functional ingredients that promise more nutrition while maintaining the taste and texture of "natural" foods. Companies such as Memphis Meats and Impossible Foods that produce meat and other protein replacements have raised impressive funds and are providing protein at affordable costs through foodservice companies, grocery stores, and school systems. Tyson foods and other former carne-centric companies have pivoted to alternative proteins, making them some of the largest sources of engineered food on the globe. But a few of Joe's customers still request animal-based pepperoni and are willing to pay a high price for their slices.

We have small, rural, soil-based farms, but they serve only the small fraction of the market that wants to pay a premium for traditionally produced food. Chefs and educators frequent these farms as a source for specialized crops and experiential programming for agricultural historians. Developing countries continue with regions of traditional farming, but urban centers now include vertical, urban farms for local distribution.

The robots have arrived gradually in this scenario. Joe interacts with fewer and fewer humans these days, and the employees that remain on his staff are paid more and aided by back-of-house robots for ingredient preparation. The repetitive tasks such as peeling, chopping, and mixing now take half as long and can be completed according to specific menu requirements, lowering the amount of food waste his shop produces. (In fact, the amount of waste in the food supply chain has dropped from 40 percent in 2018 to just 25 percent, thanks to more effective production, distribution, and portioning.) The few humans he retains work in the front of house, baking pizzas as a form of entertainment and as validation that Joe's pies are still the authentic, Sicilian kind. One human lingers by the scanner that takes payments in case a customer has failed to recharge his or her iPhone or a "paper jam" occurs, such as a power outage. Everyone else was laid off when the robot food prep system was installed a few years ago, but Joe participates in a workforce-retraining program funded by a small surcharge for his pizzas. In most cases, his former employees have found work as coders at Sysco or in smaller companies that specialize in building robots for food service companies.

Joe's dine-in customers demand more than just pizzas, now. They expect an experience, and the ambience inside evokes Sicily, with colors, music, and activities that create an environment consistent with Joe's brand. But the experience consists of more than décor. In addition to enjoying their pizza, customers use digital devices, such as tablets embedded in Joe's furnishings or their own personal devices, to buy transit tickets, order groceries, and send emails. They use VR headsets to visit with Sicilian pizza bakers or wander through the olive groves of Tuscany. They are immersed in the world Joe creates.

Some customers do still want a quick slice for their train rides to the suburbs. They order online through Joe's shop portal, and the privatized train company that took over services from Amtrak has the slice delivered to the car assigned to the customer, packaged in self-reheating, bio-compostable containers.

Food Movements

Joe doesn't have to worry about ingredients as much anymore now that he can get frequent, just-in-time deliveries at lower costs. Between the drones, AVs, and lighter-weight shipments available today, delivery vehicles have far more mobility and use much less energy. And those deliveries are safer, too, as each item is scanned multiple times throughout its journey, using predictive software to assure Joe that his ingredients meet food safety requirements and that producers grow food in response to consumer demand. This predictive approach will eliminate food waste, even lowering the amount of food that arrives in food banks.

During the past decade, new ways of managing temperatures in the cold chain became available, and these new, less costly technologies began replacing the diesel-powered coolers attached to trucks. Warehouse companies now have smaller warehouses closer to cities, a new generation of software and hardware (including robots), and renewable energy sources. Waste from the food prep station goes directly into Joe's biofuel processor, which has enabled him to operate off the NYC electrical grid for three years now. Sometimes he produces more fuel and electricity than he needs, and he sells the excess to other power grids, augmenting his revenue.

Grocery stores are some of the biggest biofuel generation hubs, using organic waste to power their warehouses and distribution centers. Food banks are turning some of their inventories into electricity. All of these bigger players join smaller operations such as Joe's in the quest for faster, cheaper delivery within an hour of purchase online. And recognition and sensing software is maturing to detect and monitor the quality and freshness of all perishables in their supply chains.

By now, Joe uses a tracking system provided by his suppliers, all of which have automated their warehouses and distribution centers. Almost half of the vehicles that deliver his ingredients and supplies are electric, a development that required him to install charging stations near his loading dock. Sysco and US Foods merged and now also operate a fleet of AVs that make weekly deliveries of flour, which is still grown in the Midwestern United States. At least one drone arrives on Sundays for both small shipments to Joe's shop and pizza deliveries to his customers in the Manhattan high-rise buildings. Only one of these deliveries has been found lying in Central Park, misdirected by out-of-date navigation software.

Tracking Our Food

In this hypothetical, evolutionary future, our food chain has emerged from its industrialized, mostly invisible state into a chain of visible, blockchain-verified transactions. Shipping ledgers have been replaced by blockchain technology, and every basil leaf now has a digital ledger entry verifying its identity and status along the pathway from farm to plate. We are buying more and more food using bitcoins, although the traditional currency system is still in place, allowing those who are risk adverse to keep their dollars in bank accounts. Still, new apps are now available that allow us to identify our food, purchase it online, and direct it to our plates for delivery.

Siri, Alexa, or whatever we want to call our personal digital assistants, can arrange for just about anything to appear on our plates for lunch, including the pizza from around the corner. The integration of AI makes it possible for these assistants to predict what we'd like to order, when we should obtain more dog food, and which new products we might want to buy from Amazon or any number of global food shopping malls. At this point, participating in data collection is optional, except for those DNA testing services. Our desire to know just how much of a Neanderthal we are means we will need to surrender our genetic data.

But in spite of the industry-wide commitment to blockchain, there are problems. Some companies resist standardizing or submitting a full accounting of events. And some submit inaccurate, poor, or dirty data, polluting the chain, creating data swamps, and causing intermittent breakdowns within the digital ledger. Efforts are underway to incentivize cooperation, but the technology is falling short of its promise of total and complete verification and tracking of all our food within the global food supply chain. It's one thing to synchronize all ingredients within the United States, but it's a fool's errand to attempt to implement the system for food produced in developing nations. While improvements have been made in the tracking and tracing of seafood across the globe, the chain of illegal fish landings persists, bound by porous trade policies and the lack of enforcement. Still, seafood is one of the first proteins that are traceable, at least through the legal supply chain. We have the capacity for tracking and tracing, but implementation is still incomplete and inconsistent.

Optimization, which we've identified as a goal for food logistics, falters despite some standardized processes that are embedded in technology. The electronic logging devices and blockchain record keeping require that we source and deliver our food according to some agreed-upon protocol. But they lack the intelligence of humans who know how to navigate a city in the early hours of the morning and are friends with the human who opens the door at just the right time, or the chef who knows a microgreen producer who just opened but is not officially in the database. What about those trusted relationships that permeated our food system in 2018 but were overruled by engineers who wanted consistent data over ad-hoc arrangements? Some engineers are pushing AI to consider real-time experiences so that exceptions can become the rule. But, in this future at least, that particular technology is still underdeveloped and remains in the lab. Scientists and engineers are beginning to realize that mapping the chemical compounds of proteins alone will take a lifetime.

The Revolutionary Future: Food 3.0

In this view, cities are smarter than ever, and Joe is living in one of the smartest cities in the world. Half of all buildings in NYC have been designed as enclosed farms. All new buildings must conform to the new specifications for rooftop gardens, integrated biogenerators, and food delivery networks. Smart kitchens are now in every kitchen designer's portfolio. Amazon's underground and blimp delivery systems are now available in four major metropolitan centers in the United States and in two cities in Asia. And Joe's pizza shop has adopted its place within the smart grid—a grid that includes energy in all forms, including calories.

What We Eat

In this revolutionary future, Joe operates within a very new food system. All of his ingredients come from no more than fifty miles away. Most of his greens and herbs come from a rooftop farm only two blocks away. He has an assigned area in the greenhouse that grows his herbs and tomatoes according to the taste profile of his customers and the ebb and flow of seasonal demand. His grain comes from another growing facility, which is outside Manhattan but still within range. (Gone are the days when grains required acres and acres of land to produce.) Now, proteins from labs manufactured at scale, produce grown in controlled environments, and vertical, underground, and aboveground farms are the norm. Dairy or dairy-like products come from a local manufacturer that uses engineered plant material that Joe can track all the way from the company's lab to his customers' to-go boxes through an iPhone app. Trucks, now all driverless, are mobile data hubs, coordinating, optimizing, and controlling the movement of food around the globe.

We've also gotten smarter about how to produce food. Food companies work with farmers to plan the quantities and production schedules. If a farmer is hit by bad weather, the producer can work with customers to adjust marketing and sourcing plans together. This increased collaboration between producers and buyers means the supply chain has fewer gaps.

For the first time, Joe has the option of buying ingredients from an orbiting agricultural farm. Yes, orbiting in space. A global space program launched in 2020 for the purpose of growing food sends shipments of lettuce and tomatoes back to earth in cargo capsules near urban depots for redistribution to cities around the world. What's more, a few artificial planets are completing their test protocols for low-altitude food production.

Back on earth, every aspect of life has become synchronized and personalized, providing entertainment and convenience at the same time. Everything is transparent. We can see our food—and ourselves—anywhere in the supply chain of everything.

Joe's customers order online with a profile containing their genetic data, a new development that allows Joe to create pizzas with personalized ingredients at a new level of integration. These customer profiles include nutritional requirements, health history, and real-time integration of physical activity. A customer can indicate a desire to lose a few pounds, signaling to Joe's system to use low-calorie tomato sauce this time. We swallow digestible sensors that monitor our own biomes, delivering information that we use to adjust our intake, eventually affecting our genetic makeup.

Pizza has always been personal, with shop menus suggesting sizes, toppings, sauces, and a multitude of additional ingredients. Personalized pizza is now precision food, designed with those same options and more. The micro-ingredient sorting is mapped to each individual customer's metabolic and nutrition genome and verified and validated using blockchain and sensors. Our entire nutritional intake is now engineered, and global life expectancy has improved by ten years or more.

Our meals take advantage of Big Data, including the data we've been accumulating on wearable devices—from smart watches to shirts made of smart fibers. We no longer need to look like compulsive athletes to capture real-time health stats; our designer blazers and smart skirts now include invisible sensors. A few of us take it even further, opting for chips embedded in our bodies, much like the older chips inserted in our pets so that we could track and trace them. The chips are useful for identification and payment systems that carry our data though sensors in our city. Smarter bodies are taking advantage of the now sophisticated and even bigger personal data networks, and AI is gradually feeling more and more like what we thought was our own intelligence. Did I mention the Singularity of Food?

All that personalized nutrition isn't limited to our pizza orders and other food we consume outside of our homes. The Big Data about health is now available to each consumer, enabling us to design our personal diets. Hospitals, clinics, schools, and other institutions that have traditionally collected and owned our data will now share it with us as our own data merges with data collected by others. We own the data and can selectively decide who uses it and how. And, for the first time, international standards making organizations have reached agreement across international borders for data gathering and processing of all food-related data, including databases that contain our health data.

We know what we can eat and how much to eat based on the activity stats in our health databases. One of the first companies to move in this direction was Habit in 2015. The startup, founded by Neil Grimmer, sent test kits to its customers that enabled them to capture information from DNA and blood samples. The data provided the customers with information about their personal requirements for nutrients, vitamins, and minerals, their ability to synthesize nutrients, and calorie requirements for weight maintenance, and it suggested meals that would fit their personal dietary profiles.

Precision agriculture has become connected to the precision health. A few of us who can afford it have personal acres on farms that produce food according to our genome and lifestyle preferences. On our iPhones, we can track our real-time health and food needs while communicating our upcoming supply needs to our producers. And those personal acres are viewable on our personal digital devices, so we can watch our own chicken as it progresses from a fluffy newborn to a nugget. We can perform a range of medical tests at home, too, now that the testing technology is easy to use, inexpensive, and practically error free. New developments in food mass spectrometry by companies such as Tellspec enable handheld scanning and testing of food. No more "best before" dates on labels, just real-time information that tells us if food is safe, authentic, and good for us.

Those of us who can't afford personal acres—and many who can—are growing some of our food at home, too. If we don't want to buy our pizza from Joe over the weekend, we may prefer making our pizza at home, from homegrown ingredients. Not a lot—just some mushrooms, microgreens, and juicy tomatoes growing in pods that fit like appliances in our smarter kitchens. They are colocated with the composting systems that turn our organic food waste into household energy. These new kitchen appliances are smart, predictive, and connected to our overall payment systems for household utilities.

It's worth noting that the old-fashioned, animal-based proteins still have their place in this revolutionary future. Food producers such as Carghill, Archer-Daniels, and Campbell's Soup Company have bought Go-Go Chicken and Cainthus, both of which brought out facial recognition for livestock in 2018.[1] The ability to visually recognize individual animals in our global food supply chain has given animal-based protein a boost in the market by making it possible to verify the welfare of each animal as it passes through the supply chain. Ethics are defined and managed now, making animal protein more acceptable to those who prefer the taste experience of animals over engineered substitutes. The cost of producing animals for food has gone down since initial investments were paid back, so animal proteins are available to all income levels. Removing food production to newer, enclosed labs and farms has largely mitigated the environmental impact of producing food in the water and on the land.

But old-fashioned proteins are no longer the dietary staple they once were. As data, connectivity, and AI have converged, it's not uncommon to find all sorts of engineered food in our food system. The anxieties over GMO foods that prevailed in the early 2000s were calmed by the arrival of gene editing technology such as CRISPR. Once consumers understood the technology as one that avoided introducing foreign genes into their food, they became comfortable letting CRISPR genetically engineer food. Once CRISPR entered the labs of food scientists and engineers, the food industry was able to adapt digital tools, including genome mapping and testing, to create foods that targeted smaller and smaller groups and ultimately individual consumers. Genetically designing and modifying our food has become the new norm, and foods can be designed in a way that makes them function more and more like medicine. If we have a disease that requires us to eat a specific ingredient, mineral, vitamin, or pharmaceutical, we obtain foods that are precisely personalized for our needs. Some would say that food is now pharma to table, instead of farm to table. As a result, our hospitals have transitioned to meditation centers, coworking spaces, and sports facilities. Chris Traeger, of the classic TV show *Parks and Recreation*, would be satisfied to know that he could live to the age of 150 just by consuming a few pizzas a week, as long as those pizzas were designed to add to his life expectancy.

Though CRISPR and similar technologies saw relatively little resistance, the big surprise is still how much food we engineer in 2030. We learned in the early twenty-first century that the demand for food, especially fresh and organic food, would outstrip our ability to produce it. For a decade, the Chinese and other countries bought up farmland in Africa and remote areas of Asia in an effort to produce enough food to meet demand. Ultimately, the startup costs were too big, the climate too changeable, and the transport costs too high to warrant a continuation of land-based food production. We moved on to engineered and manufactured food as we depleted wild resources and traditional farms.

Of course, engineered food had a rough beginning. In 2015, 3-D printed pizzas met skeptical consumers who informed hopeful engineers that printed pizzas would not be competitive with the human-made pies. People just lost interest in the thin, painted crust that lacked bubbly cheese, some laid down in irregular patterns, and the texture of tomatoes that were imperfectly chopped and processed into sauce.

Engineers sometimes forget that the complicated relationship of humans and their food includes sensation, emotion, and culture. Our relationship is not entirely rational, and thus a rational design for anything, even non-food, in our food system often stumbles or fails to capture human trust and acceptance. Remember Soylent, the drinkable food created by engineers who couldn't be bothered to stop working in order to prepare a meal? Instead, they argued, drinking a processed, nutritionally optimized beverage would satisfy us. Well, it worked for a few workaholics, but the market largely rejected it, and products pivoted to the emerging personalized health market with drinkable food matched to our genome. Even the claim that drinkable meal replacements such as Soylent are better for the environment failed to overcome the need some customers feel for a "real" pizza. Though, in all honesty, the notion of "real" has changed, too. The new proteins from labs—and even the insect- and algae-based proteins that remain a staple of our diets—have achieved a level of acceptance that makes them seem somehow "real."

In this hyper-connected, engineered future, our personal health data and diets shape how everyone sells food to us. Groceries include smart—really smart—sensors that can drive us to the right food items that match our profile, not just in a demographic sense but in a medical and physical sense. Some grocery sensors know our emotional dispositions and suggest a pint of ice cream if we need comforting.

Food Movements

In developing countries, more well off than in 2019, mobile grocery stores have appeared, as have pop-up mobile storage and processing facilities that have made food more accessible to poor and drought-prone regions. The World Food Programme has begun to work as a network of pop-up microproduction and distribution centers, abandoning the food aid programs that had sent food in bulk thousands of miles to areas of conflict. Now, regions in crisis have begun to develop their own local sourcing areas in secure locations. Blockchain technology provides both secure identities and transactions for the procurement of food and distribution to refugee populations.

Food banks, long a fixture in developed countries as a way to distribute potential food waste to poor communities, have disappeared. Instead, predictive analytics and AI have enabled precise coordination among producers and grocery stores and the food service industry, eliminating the need for the food banks to collect and distribute food. As growers produce food in quantities more aligned with real-time demand, food service and grocery stores now do their own distribution of food to poor communities. Imagine

Instacart or Postmates with delivery vehicles that contain food for both the rich and the poor, free or priced for both the haves and have nots.

In 2019, grocery stores, like shopping malls and other brick-and-mortar retail stores, were realizing that business would not be as usual going forward. They watched as their customers ordered more sugar and flour online and engaged Instacart and other delivery companies to deliver their orders. Some grocery chains had their own delivery services, but e-commerce forced them to rethink their business platforms and begin designing their physical shopping spaces as experiences rather than transaction spaces. Even clothing stores began to add their equivalent of "grocerants," restaurants within grocery stores.

In the developed world, grocery stores were already well on their way to transforming their stores with additions of grocerants, cooking classes, and pickup boxes where customers could swing by to pick up their online orders. In our Revolutionary Future, those changes have become widespread, with grocery stores adding other experiences such as dry cleaning, spa treatments, and banking. Grocery stores become experience hubs. Places where families or groups of friends come to spend time together—and maybe pick up a loaf of bread and a case of beer. Grocery stores incorporate many of the old mall experiences under their own roofs, allowing for more social engagement, meet-ups, and performances—without the soulless feel of malls and with all the excitement of the old food halls of Victorian England.

In addition to enjoying the experiential treatment, customers now can shop in smart shops with heads-up displays that tell them about the food on the shelves: carbon footprint, nutrition, health, origins, producers, genetics, labor practices, and just about anything we'd like to know in the new era of ultra-transparency. Shoppers can personally select the items they want, and the orders will be picked, packed, and sent to their homes without any further action required—not even a trip to the checkout stand. That's right, facial recognition and product scanners make it possible to eliminate all the old checkout counters. Amazon discovered that consumers would rather enter a humanless grocery store way back in 2016. So now we have Autonomous Stores (AS). Those stores that still serve humans in person will rely on our faces for scans that indicate our food preferences and the inventory in our kitchens back home. So instead of waiting in line, we can linger in the grocery's spa for a pedicure. When we get home, we can bring our food in from its cooled container outside and give it a quick scan for safety unless the delivery service has already done that for us.

We can shop at farmers' markets for those mushrooms grown by humans in spaces that operate with municipal funds from parks and recreation budgets. Those food producers don't need to generate a profit since they are underwritten by the city for their contributions to the education and aesthetic environment of city dwellers.

Serious grocery shopping, though, is mostly done through delivery services. Joe's patrons use specialized services for fresh food, meat, eggs, and produce. Each service utilizes personal data and provides convenience, transparency, and storytelling on an individualized basis. We want food designed for our own taste? These delivery services work through their own platforms or as part of a grocery chain that will aggregate fresh orders with the staples offered in brick-and-mortar stores. Consumers have choices for food delivered as meals, ingredients, or—for a steep premium—by a chef who comes to their home to prepare that evening's meal.

By the way, all that packaging that once enclosed our ingredients, filled trashcans, and left environmentalists tearing their hair out? That's changed, too. Almost all food packaging is integrated into the ingredients, protecting and conserving them all along the supply chain. Apples sealed in invisible edible skins impervious to contamination, meat packaged in protective edible sheaths. Edible packaging will mean that we can make other ingredients from the ingredients in the wrappers or compost them in our vegetable garden. The few packages that remain exist to contain bulk shipments and are fully repurposed in other food or animal products or, of course, integrated into an energy generation network embedded in our city. Portions are designed to fit demand, whether according to personal dietary needs or by market demand.

In fact, landfills are languishing as organic food waste is directed toward energy generation facilities and other compostable material, such as packaging, is repurposed into building materials and consumer goods. Garbage cans previously positioned at the end of our driveways are long gone, as composted organic material powers our homes. (By the way, these days, there's not much food waste anymore. Just 10 percent of what we produce—and we reuse all of it to generate power and make new products like clothing.)

Localized warehouses will deliver bulk staples in a range of vehicles, from post office AVs to UPS drones. Consumers can also choose to drive by a store at their convenience to pick up orders that have been picked, packed, and placed in drive-through areas with accessible pickup boxes. These grocery stores left their large interest group lobbies, such as the Grocery Manufacturers Association, so they could act more independently to respond to the availability of new technologies and the rapidly changing marketplace. AVs have no need to park since they are designed to be always on the move. We (or our personal AVs) travel to grocery stores, or the AVs travel to us, eliminating food deserts by delivering fresh food customized to our neighborhoods when and where we need it. Some of the grocery stores are growing produce on their own flat roofs and in container farms in their abandoned parking lots.

Packaged goods and other goods and services flow smoothly into the online delivery supply chain, but fresh food has been sticky and complicated. Partnerships in Europe between food retailers and companies similar to Ocado keep Europe, Asia, and even Africa ahead of the United States with innovations for food delivery and supply chain innovations. Cities such as Singapore had been far ahead of Europe and the United States when it came to Last Mile delivery technology, and they now continue to pioneer the most advanced of food delivery technologies.

As grocery stores changed, so did the transportation infrastructure. Sometimes, the global food network is contained almost entirely in the cloud. For example, Joe now has customers in Hong Kong, Kenya, London, and Sydney, and he has Cloud Kitchens that can produce New York slices customized to local cultures and delivered by AVs within an hour of online ordering. These Cloud Kitchens enable food brands to extend their markets without building any dine-in structures.

Closer to home, over half of all vehicles now use electricity or hybrid electric/gas, and half the vehicles on the road are AVs designed especially for freight transport. The effect of this transition is enormous, and one impact is the changing role of gas stations. By 2018, Reebok and the design company Gensler had already reimagined how gas stations would become recharging stations—not only for vehicles but also for people.[2] Reebok reconceived the old gas station as one that had a few gas pumps but more charging stations, a farm-to-table hub, an exercise center, a yoga studio, meditation spaces, and a coworking center for meetings and collaborative projects.

Truck drivers like the ones who drop off Joe's ingredients no longer worry about the future of their jobs. In some senses, they were right in 2018:

AVs, robots, and drones are commonplace as petroleum and coal supplies became too expensive—not to mention illegal—due to commitments made by the international community. Still, however, demand for drivers (though they might be more aptly called "vehicle supervisors" now) has actually grown along with e-commerce, and trucking companies are enlarging their fleets, driving in pelotons, drafting while conserving energy, and carrying full loads. In the past, governments had been trying to lubricate the adoption of technology by sidestepping the workforce implications of replacing human intelligence with artificial intelligence, but old industries—like trucking—with long histories of powerful labor unions continued to put up significant resistance. Unfortunately, in many cases, that resistance has backfired, as the more unions bargained for higher pay the more the industry moved to integrate robots into the food system. These unions have had better luck aligning themselves with regions and urban centers, finding ways to allow for innovation and technology while mitigating the issues of job loss and workforce fragmentation. Many of the unions are gone, realizing that the labor force replaced the bargaining power of unions in the past with new tech tools that have removed barriers between management and labor. Still, the effect of the transition from humans to digital tools has left many workers struggling to retool their skills for this future.

Though Joe sells more slices than ever, hardly anyone actually comes into his shop, except for a few commuters who use the electric car chargers at the new PennRecharge Center located in a transport hub that organizes the subterranean mobile system. The system, operated by a partnership between Google and Amazon, sends food, humans, waste, and energy throughout the city in an underground network. Those ugly dumpsters and double-parked tractor-trailers no longer infringe upon our enjoyment of our new, smarter cities. What's more, apartments and condominiums are now built with integrated, temperature-controlled boxes that are accessible indoors and outdoors for food deliveries. Joe's shop even has its own cold storage boxes that are accessible from the street and through Amazon's underground food tubes and conveyor belts so delivery drivers no longer have to wander through the aisles in his back room to find the cold locker. The need for outsiders to enter our homes and businesses for food deliveries has gone by the wayside, so we can feel perfectly secure ordering that pizza in time to find it waiting for us when we get home from work. Energy-wise, the city is a closed, sustainable system.

Tracking Our Food

Joe's Pizza Suprema remains in its familiar location outside Penn Station, a locus of charging stations, AVs, drone landing pads, and light rail service. New York's power grids now include energy production through conversion of organic waste, water systems, and vertical farms. Joe can now track food shipments, adjust deliveries, and use sensors to detect concerns for food safety and allergens just before consumption.

Although truckers resisted tracking technology in 2019, the drivers who deliver Joe's ingredients today now belong to an Internet of AVs (IoAV), which is informed by machine learning software. Over the past years, these new digital platforms for trucking companies have offered individual truckers the freedom to use data about optimum times for access to buildings, parking options, wait times, and demand for products.

The boxes that fill these trucks resemble the old shipping containers. But these are "smart" boxes that know where they are in real time and know how to keep their internal temperatures—all of them—at the right level, signaling when organic contents have begun to oxidize. These smart boxes travel on water, roads, and through the underground conveyors and tubes that operate beneath the city streets, but thanks to the enhanced connectivity of the IoT and the IoAV (the Internet of Everything, really), these boxes and their contents are visible onscreen every step of the way.

And tracking isn't just for commercial food, either. At home, we now have very smart kitchens. If we're in doubt about a food's properties, we can test it at home a few seconds before we place that suspect shellfish casserole on our plate. AI and VR inhabit our kitchens, too. Our coffee maker knows when to order more beans. The fridge can tell us when an item spoils and when to order more milk. Our cooktop uses biofuel produced from our composter and will regulate itself according to temperature and time for the foods on the cooktop and in the oven. We shop in grocery stores that are virtually represented through flat screens projected on our kitchen walls, enabling us to meander through store aisles as we receive data about individual banana ripeness and related sensorial characteristics of fresh produce. We can order and interact with the store from our kitchens if we exist in both places at one time. All of this smartness creates a seamless, transparent supply chain, using both cryptocurrencies and blockchain to track food from around the world through the networks in our own kitchens.

Evolution or Revolution: Where Do We Fit In?

Still, the persistence of the human desire for connection through the senses and community could not be entirely replaced by engineered food, robots, and drones. The effect of the advances of more and more tech in food was an increase of the perceived value of low- or no-tech food. Handcrafted pizza, personal delivery, and the restaurant concierge who lingers over a description of wine or lamb chops have become the high end of food service. There still is some resistance by those consumers who desire the presence of humans and the organic substance of soil and the physical sensations related to the earth, plants, animals, and us. There's still a market for those producers, and their customers pay more for the pleasure of human-grown food.

As they became detached from natural habitats, our food production systems moved closer to consumers, where they could take advantage of scale and customization and become much more environmentally sustainable. While it seemed at first that we were returning to Big Food and an industrialized food system, we realized that through technology that enabled full transparency and trust, bigness became an acceptable route to affordable and accessible food. Fewer big distribution centers serve more localized, regional distribution centers that send smaller shipments to individual customers.

In both futures, most of us live in cities, and our food system has had to adapt. Our homes are smaller, integrated into smart grids, and near localized distribution hubs. We have cold-chain storage in small spaces, like street reefers and condo cold chains, all with smaller footprints and energy consumption.

Not many of us have gone back to the kitchen in the way Alice Waters and Dan Barber had hoped. We cook, yes, but only once in a while, more as an experience with friends—a social activity. And most of our ingredients have been prepared ahead of time. Sliced onions, peeled carrots. Our ingredients are fresher than they were in 2018, since we now have better packaging and most of the food we get is grown locally, only minimally processed, and not stored for long en route. Convenience has trumped tradition in our return to the kitchen.

We now have many more options for food, and we use them all: one day we order out from our favorite fried chicken shop, using its private delivery service. The next, we join our friends at their house for hamburgers made of plant-based protein, which tastes delicious once grilled and placed between two buns made from potatoes and proto-grains. AI has enabled food shopping and delivery to sense our moods and inform our food choices.

All the scenarios included in both the Evolutionary and Revolutionary Futures point to a food system and supply chain that is digitally connected, sharing platforms and merging data into one Big Data system. Food is a complicated subject for futurists for all the reasons suggested in this book— its connection to our humanness, identity, senses, and social and cultural relationships. Because food bridges the boundaries between technology and art, humans and machines, we still need to think smartly about the consequences of these imagined futures for our food system. How do we preserve our individuality and humanness, and how can we opt out of the system and still operate within a highly connected society? As Art Markman once asked me, "What in our food system can't be automated?" We wonder how important the five senses will be in our future. We're about to enter unknown territory in terms of the latest Industrial Revolution. Major breakthroughs in biotechnology, AI, and machine learning are rapidly appearing, and we don't have time to see how they will play out in our lives (except possibly on TV in *Black Mirror)*. We can imagine the consequences but have little evidence yet of our new reality.

Will our engineered food miss a humanness that is imagined now but real in the future? We wonder how we will rationalize the move of technology into our food system. We're already rationalizing CRISPR technology as an acceptable means for genetically engineering food; and making meat out of animal cells in a lab, perhaps the most extreme form of processing, is acceptable to those who eschewed processed food in their diets. The tools we will develop to make the food system transparent will provide trust to those who were skeptical of industrialized food. We know the engineer in the lab and have replaced the intimate relationship with a rural farmer with that of the young engineer who labors over a petri dish in Santa Monica. We write ourselves new stories to make our new food landscape compatible with our sense of ethics and humanness.

Many of the institutions and silos that exist today will continue their evolution from big to small, from centralized to distributed in how they perform their services and produce their products. Health care, finance, agriculture, and every traditional industry that has operated big and deep will finally have new communities, and the data that was traditionally guarded and developed within the boundaries of those sectors will begin moving closer to consumers. They have demanded more control of their lives in a society that has continued to be more fragmented and unpredictable.

But even the older technology miracles haven't worked out all the kinks yet. Digital printers have been around since the 1950s, but we still stop to remove sheets of paper that jam our work progress.

What will be the "paper jam" in our food logistics' future? Will terrorists benefit from full transparency of our food supply chain? Will our lives become overstandardized as we do the same things every day to accommodate the needs of our digital processors? Will AI and VR remove us from our present moment? Will our humanness eventually rebel against convenience? Probably.

Stand back. Our food is being rerouted.

Notes

Chapter 1

1. Antoine Henri Jomini, George H. Mendell, and Wm. P. Craighill. *The Art of War* (San Francisco, CA: Sublime Books, 2015), 148.

2. OECD Data, "Meat Consumption," 2016, https://data.oecd.org/agroutput/meat-consumption.htm.

3. "The Decade Ahead: Trends That Will Shape the Consumer Goods Industry," McKinsey & Company, 2010, 5.

4. "News Flash: September 18, 2014," NIOP, October 13, 2014, accessed July 10, 2017, http://www.niop.org/news-flash-september-18-2014; Brian Cross, "Clogged: Logistics Leave Farmers in the Cold," *Western Producer*, March 7, 2014, accessed July 10, 2017, http://www.producer.com/2014/03/clogged-logistics-leave-farmers-in-the-cold.

5. Jacob Bunge, "Organic Food Sales Are Booming; Why Are American Farmers Crying Foul?" last modified Feb. 21, 2017, www.wsj.com/articles/u-s-appetite-for-organic-food-prompts-jump-in-grain-imports-farmers-cry-foul-1487673002?mg=prod/accounts-wsj.

6. Greg Knowler, "New Korean Connection Expands China-Europe Rail Service," June 29, 2017, https://www.joc.com/rail-intermodal/international-rail/asia/new-korean-connection-expands-china-europe-rail-service_20170629.html

Chapter 2

1. Chris Brown, "Sanctions Present Russian Cheesemakers with Gouda Opportunity," August 14, 2017, http://www.cbc.ca/news/world/russia-cheese-economy-1.4243222.

2. Steve Martinez et al., "Local Food Systems: Concepts, Impacts, and Issues," USDA ERS, accessed July 12, 2017, https://permanent.access.gpo.gov/lps125302/ERR97.pdf.

3. "NYC Regional Foodshed Initiative," Urban Design Lab, NYC Regional Foodshed Initiative Comments, accessed July 12, 2017, http://urbandesignlab.columbia.edu/projects/food-and-the-urban-environment/nyc-regional-food-shed-initiative.

4. Ibid

5. Colin K. Khoury et al., "Origins of food crops connect countries worldwide," *Proceedings of the Royal Society*, June 2016, accessed July 12, 2017, http://rspb.royal societypublishing.org/content/283/1832/20160792.

6. Jean-Paul Rodrique and Theo Notteboom. "Transport Costs." *The Geography of Transport Systems,* https://transportgeography.org/?page_id=5268.

7. David Coley, Mark Howard, and Michael Winter, "Local Food, Food Miles and Carbon Emissions: A Comparison of Farm Shop and Mass Distribution Approaches," *Food Policy*, 34, no. 2, April 2009, 150–155.

8. Steven Sexton, "Does Local Production Improve Environmental and Health Outcomes?," https://s.giannini.ucop.edu/uploads/giannini_public/f3/15/f3158a2d-374e -4513-86e5-30a8c9f393a0/v13n2_2.pdf, 6; "Agriculture's Supply and Demand for Energy and Energy Products," USDA ERS, May 2013, accessed July 12, 2017, https:// www.ers.usda.gov/publications/pub-details/?pubid=43757;   Christine   Wallgren, "Local or Global Food Markets: A Comparison of Energy Use for Transport," *Local Environment* 11, no. 2 (2006): 233–251; J.N. Pretty, A.S. Ball, T. Lang, and J.I.L. Morison, "Farm Costs and Food Miles: An Assessment of the Full Cost of the UK Weekly Food Basket," *Food Policy* 30, no. 1 (2005), 1–19, http://www.sciencedirect.com/science/ article/pii/S0306919205000059.

9. Alex A. Avery, and Dennis T. Avery, "The Local Organic Food Paradigm," *Georgetown Journal of International Affairs* 9, no. 1 (2008): 33–40, http://www.jstor.org .ezproxy.lib.utexas.edu/stable/43134165.

10. Rich Pirog and Nick McCann, "Is Local Food More Expensive? A Consumer Price Perspective on Local and Non-Local Foods Purchased in Iowa," Leopold Center for Sustainable Agriculture, Iowa State University, December 2009, http://www.agmrc .org/media/cms/Is_Local_Food_More_Expensive_0DEEF5B9A5323.pdf.

11. "Overview of the United States Dairy Industry," National Agricultural Statistics Service, September 22, 2010, http://usda.mannlib.cornell.edu/usda/current/ USDairyIndus/USDairyIndus-09-22-2010.pdf; "Agricultural Production and Prices," USDA ERS, last updated May 5, 2017, https://www.ers.usda.gov/data-products/ ag-and-food-statistics-charting-the-essentials/agricultural-production-and-prices.

12. Arama Kukutai and Spencer Maughan, "How the Agtech Investment Boom Will Create a Wave of Agriculture Unicorns," *Forbes*, January 16, 2018, accessed January 20, 2018, https://www.forbes.com/sites/outofasia/2018/01/16/how-the-agtech -investment-boom-will-create-a-wave-of-agriculture-unicorns/#598e1f11562b.

13. MIT Open Phenome Project, accessed June 5, 2017, https://www.media.mit .edu/research/groups/open-phenome-project.

14. Andrew Haughwout, James Orr, and David Bedoll, "The Price of Land in the New York Metropolitan Area," *Current Issues in Economics and Finance* 14, no. 3, (April/May 2008), https://www.newyorkfed.org/medialibrary/media/research/current_issues/ ci14-3.pdf.

15. Wendong Zhang, "2016 Farmland Value Survey," Iowa State University, accessed July 18, 2017, https://www.extension.iastate.edu/AGDM/wholefarm/html/ c2-70.html.

16. Farm Credit Administration, Roundtable on Farm Real Estate, "Land Values: Current and Future Prospects," accessed March 20, 2017, https://www.fca.gov/Download/FarmlandValuePresentations/GloyRoundtablePresentation.pdf; The Federal Reserve Bank of New York, "The Price of Land in the New York Metropolitan Area, 14, no. 3 (April/May 2008), accessed March 20, 2017, https://www.nrc.gov/docs/ML1233/ML12334A798.pdf.

17. "About Us," Gotham Greens, http://gothamgreens.com/our-story.

18. Freight Farms website, https://www.freightfarms.com/features.

19. "Our Story," AeroFarms, http://aerofarms.com/story.

20. "Who We Are," Local Roots, www.localrootsfarms.com.

21. "First Large-Scale Commercial Vertical Farm in Europe to Be Set Up in the Netherlands." Produce Grower. February 10, 2017, accessed August 2017, http://www.producegrower.com/article/philips-lighting-vertical-farm-netherlands.

22. Philip K. Thornton, "Livestock Production: Recent Trends, Future Prospects," *Philosophical Transactions B*, 365 (1554): 2853–2867, accessed June 2017, http://rstb.royalsocietypublishing.org/content/365/1554/2853.

23. "Meat the Team," Memphis Meats, http://www.memphismeats.com/the-team.

24. Daniela Galarza, "Lab-Grown Meat Finally Available in Chicken Nugget Form," Eater.com, March 15, 2017, https://www.eater.com/2017/3/15/14933922/lab-grown-chicken-duck-memphis-meats.

25. "Memphis Meats Announces World's First 'Clean Poultry,'" Memphis Meats press release, March 15, 2017, https://static1.squarespace.com/static/5674c0c22399a3a13cbc3af2/t/58c94becff7c508dcd28b8ff/1489587181184/Memphis+Meats+-+Press+Release+15+Mar+2017+Final.pdf.

26. Lindsey Hoshaw, "Silicon Valley's Bloody Plant Burger Smells, Tastes and Sizzles Like Meant," NPR, June 21, 2016, http://www.npr.org/sections/thesalt/2016/06/21/482322571/silicon-valley-s-bloody-plant-burger-smells-tastes-and-sizzles-like-meat.

27. D. Dobermann, J. A. Swift, and L. M. Field, "Opportunities and hurdles of edible insects for food and feed," *Nutrition Bulletin* 42, no. 4 (November 10, 2017): 293–308, doi:10.1111/nbu.12291.

28. Dana Perls, "Is 'Food Tech' the Future of Food?," Medium, March 30, 2017, https://medium.com/@foe_us/is-food-tech-the-future-of-food-49bd414cfb8b.

29. V. V. Tijare et al., "Meat Quality of Broiler Breast Fillets With White Striping and Woody Breast Muscle Myopathies," *Poultry Science* 95, no. 9 (2016): 2167–2173, https://academic.oup.com/ps/article/95/9/2167/2223517

30. Aviagen, http://en.aviagen.com; "Aviagen to Appoint North American General Manager for Slower-Growing Poultry Segment," Aviagen press release, January 30, 2017, http://en.aviagen.com/aviagen-to-appoint-north-american-general-manager-for-slower-growing-poultry-market-segment; Chase Purdy, "After Years of Designing Fatter Birds, Food Companies Are Finally Realizing Chickens Shouldn't Grow So Fast," Quartz, March 1, 2017, https://qz.com/922309/how-chicken-farming

-works-and-why-companies-like-whole-foods-wfm-chipotle-cmg-and-tyson-foods
-tsn-are-now-realizing-chickens-shouldnt-grow-so-fast.

31. "USDA Defines Food Deserts," *American Nutrition Association's Nutrition Digest* 38, no. 2, accessed July 12, 2017, http://americannutritionassociation.org/newsletter/ usda-defines-food-deserts.

32. Hillary J. Shaw, "Food Deserts: Towards the Development of a Classification," *Geografiska Annaler Series B, Human Geography* 88, no. 2 (2006): 231–247.

33. Marianne Bitler and Steven J. Haider, "An Economic View of Food Deserts in the United States," *Journal of Policy Analysis and Management* 30, no. 1 (New York, Modern Library, 2010): 153–176.

34. K. C. Abel, and K. M. Faust, "Modeling Food Desert Disruptors: An Object Oriented Programming Approach," presented at Canadian Society for Civil Engineering (CSCE) Annual Conference and General Meeting, Vancouver, British Colombia, May 31–June 2, 2017, 9.

35. "How to Feed the World in 2050," FAO, http://www.fao.org/fileadmin/templates/ wsfs/docs/expert_paper/How_to_Feed_the_World_in_2050.pdf.

36. "Agriculture Production and Prices," USDA ERS. Sharing the Economic Burden: Who Pays for WIC's Infant Formula. Accessed August 2, 2018. https://www.ers.usda .gov/data-products/ag-and-food-statistics-charting-the-essentials/agricultural -production-and-prices.aspx.

37. "The State of Food and Agriculture 2014: In Brief," FAO, 2014, http://www.fao .org/3/a-i4036e.pdf.

38. "2012 Census Highlights," USDA Census of Agriculture, May 2014, https://www .agcensus.usda.gov/Publications/2012/Online_Resources/Highlights/Farm_Demo graphics.

Chapter 3

1. Eve Adamson, "Michael Pollan: Three Simple Rules for Eating," Stronger Together. coop, accessed July 19, 2017, http://strongertogether.coop/food-lifestyle/michael -pollan-three-simple-rules-for-eating.

2. For an illustration of the meatpacking district in Buenos Aires, see Aldolfo Bellocq's *Meat Packers*, woodcut, 1922.

3. "Doritos 'Party in Your Mouth,'" Vimeo, February 15, 2018, vimeo.com/ 146040535.

4. Carrie Lock, "Original Microbrews," *Science News* 166, no. 14 (2004): 216–218.

5. Sara J. Risch, "Food Packaging History and Innovations," *Journal of Agricultural and Food Chemistry* 57 (2009), 8089–8092, http://www.pfigueiredo.org/Emb_19.pdf.

6. Milner Gray, "The History and Development of Packaging," *Journal of the Royal Society of Arts* 87, no. 4511 (1939): 633–658.

7. "IceWrap," Maxwell Chase Technologies, LLC, accessed July 19, 2017, http://www .maxwellchase.com/icewrap.

8. Olive R. Jones, "Commercial Foods, 1740–1820," *Historical Archaeology* 27, no. 2 (1993): 25–41.

9. Sharon Durham, "Food 'Tattoos': An Alternative to Labels for Identifying Fruit," US Department of Agriculture, Agricultural Research Service, August 31, 2009, https://www.ars.usda.gov/news-events/news/research-news/2009/food-quottattoosquot-an-alternative-to-labels-for-identifying-fruit.

10. CFR—Code of Federal Regulations, Title 21, US Food & Drug Administration, last updated September 21, 2016, https://www.accessdata.fda.gov/scripts/cdrh/cfdocs/cfcfr/CFRSearch.cfm?fr=179.43

11. Ibid.

12. "WikiFoods," Quantum Designs, accessed July 19, 2017, http://quantumdesigns.com/wikifoods.

13. Apeel Sciences, http://apeelsciences.com/index.html.

14. R. K. Dhall, "Advances in Edible Coatings for Fresh Fruits and Vegetables: A Review," *Critical Reviews in Food Science and Nutrition* 53, no. 5 (2013), http://www.tandfonline.com/doi/abs/10.1080/10408398.2010.541568; Sabina Galus, Justyna Kadzińska, "Food applications of emulsion-based edible films and coatings, *Trends in Food Science & Technology* 45, no. 2, 2015, 273–283, accessed July 3, 2017, http://www.sciencedirect.com/science/article/pii/S0924224415001788)

15. The Associated Press, "Molasses Kills Nine," *Washington Post*, January 16, 1919.

16. "12 Killed When Tank of Molasses Explodes," *New York Times*, January 16, 1919.

17. Stephen Puleo, *Dark Tide*, (Boston: Beacon Press, 2004), 89–141.

18. "Crops," Food and Agriculture Organization of the United Nations, accessed July 20, 2017, http://www.fao.org/faostat/en/#data/QC; Thomas J. Goldsby, "A Comparative Analysis of Agricultural Transportation and Logistics Systems in the United States and Argentina," MATRIC Research Paper 00-MRP 3, August 2000, http://ageconsearch.umn.edu/bitstream/18694/1/rp000003.pdf.

19. "Industry News," Prologis, accessed July 20, 2017, https://www.prologis.com/logistics-industry-news.

20. Arnold Maltz, "Amazon Is Going Underwater. Seriously," *Fortune*, July 23, 2017, http://fortune.com/2017/07/23/amazon-underwater-storage-facility/

21. Thijs Defraeye et al., "Towards integrated performance evaluation of future packaging for fresh produce in the cold chain," *Trends in Food Science & Technology* 44, no. 2 (2015), 201–225, http://www.sciencedirect.com/science/article/pii/S0924224415001016.

22. "Let's Glean!," USDA United We Serve Toolkit, https://www.usda.gov/sites/default/files/documents/usda_gleaning_toolkit.pdf.

23. Imperfect Produce, accessed January 2017, www.imperfectproduce.com.

24. Kroger press release, http://www.feedresource.org/KR-RS-press-release.pdf; Megan Greenwalt, "How One Massachusetts Grocer Is Converting Food Waste to Energy," Waste360, May 4, 2016, http://www.waste360.com/anaerobic-digestion/how-one-massachusetts-grocer-converting-food-waste-energy; Roger Beliveau and Kristina

Stefanski, "Stop & Shop Freetown Anaerobic Digester Slide Presentation for MADEP," http://www.mass.gov/eea/docs/dep/public/committee-4/stopshop.pdf.

25. RenGen Villages, http://www.regenvillages.com.

26. Kristen A. Schmitt, "Turning Food Waste into a Fashion Statement," *National Geographic*, May 31, 2016, http://www.nationalgeographic.com/people-and-culture/food/the-plate/2016/05/turning-food-waste-into-a-fashion-statement.

27. "Introducing Pinatex," Ananas Anam, accessed June 12, 2017. http://www.ananas-anam.com/pinatex.

28. Bekah Wright, "From Coffee Grounds to Couture, Food Waste Turns Into Fashion," *Design + Innovation*, May 23, 2106, http://www.takepart.com/feature/2016/05/23/food-upcycling-fashions.

Chapter 4

1. "Growth in the Nation's Freight Shipments: Highlights," Bureau of Transportation Statistics, accessed July 20, 2017, https://www.rita.dot.gov/bts/sites/rita.dot.gov.bts/files/publications/freight_shipments_in_america/html/entire.html.

2. Jean-Paul Rodrigue, "Historical Geography of Transportation: The Emergence of Mechanized Systems," Hofstra University website, accessed July 20, 2017, https://people.hofstra.edu/geotrans/eng/ch2en/conc2en/ch2c1en.html.

3. "Reports, Trends & Statistics," American Trucking Association, 11, accessed July 20, 2017, http://www.trucking.org/News_and_Information_Reports_Industry_Data.aspx.

4. Peloton Technology, https://peloton-tech.com.

5. "Reebok Reimagines Gas Stations," NACS, January 18, 2018, http://www.convenience.org/Media/Daily/Pages/ND0118182_Reebok-Reimagines-Gas-Stations.aspx#_ga=2.247965319.1284170930.1517499887-14175973.1517499887.

6. "Uber Seen Raising Bar for Truck Freight Brokerage," *Trucking Logistics,* April 7, 2017, http://www.joc.com/trucking-logistics/uber-seen-raising-bar-truck-freight-brokerage_20170407.html; David H. Freeman, "Self-Driving Trucks," *MIT Technology Review*, February 22, 2017, https://www.technologyreview.com/s/603493/10-breakthrough-technologies-2017-self-driving-trucks.

7. "State of Trucking for 2017: The Driver Shortage," *Heavy Duty Trucking*, December 2, 2016, http://www.truckinginfo.com/channel/drivers/news/story/2016/12/state-of-trucking-for-2017.aspx.

8. Drew McElroy, "What Tesla's Semi Truck Says about the Future of Trucking," Supply Chain Dive, January 9, 2018, https://www.supplychaindive.com/news/Tesla-Elon-Musk-electric-autonomous-semi-truck-freight/514315/

9. "Freight Rail and Agriculture: Feeding the World," Association of American Railroads, accessed August 2, 2017, https://www.aar.org/wp-content/uploads/2018/03/AAR-Agriculture-Issue.pdf.

10. Federal Railroad Administration, "Freight Rail Overview," US Department of Transportation, accessed July 20, 2017, https://www.fra.dot.gov/Page/P0362.

11. Edwin Lopez and Jennifer McKevitt, "Train Length Increases in Effort to Keep Costs Down, Efficiency Up," Supply Chain Dive, July 7, 2017, http://www .supplychaindive.com/news/freight-train-length-carrier-market-cost-service/446410.

12. FASonline, https://apps.fas.usda.gov/export-sales/myrkmay.htm.

13. "Lock Performance Monitoring System," US Army Corps of Engineers, accessed July 20, 2017, http://corpslocks.usace.army.mil/lpwb/f?p=121:6:0::NO.

14. JOC Staff, "Slideshow: Top Waves Hitting Ocean Shippers in 2017," *Journal of Commerce*, January 16, 2017, http://www.joc.com/maritime-news/slide-show-top -waves-hitting-ocean-shippers-2017_20170109.html?page=0%2C2.

15. "Chapter 1: Air Cargo—An Historical Perspective," Airports Council International— North America, accessed July 20, 2017, http://www.aci-na.org/sites/default/files/ chapter_1_-_an_historical_perspective.pdf.

16. Office of the Historian, "The Berlin Airlift, 1948–1949," US Department of State, accessed July 20, 2017, https://history.state.gov/milestones/1945-1952/berlin-airlift.

17. Adrienne Wilmoth Lerner, "Berlin Airlift," *Encyclopedia of Espionage, Intelligence, and Security,* Encyclopedia.com, July 21, 2017, http://www.encyclopedia.com/history/ modern-europe/german-history/berlin-airlift.

18. "World Air Cargo Forecast," Boeing, accessed July 20, 2017, http://www.boeing .com/commercial/market/cargo-forecast.

19. "GDP Growth, Annual %," World Bank, accessed July 20, 2017, http://data .worldbank.org/indicator/NY.GDP.MKTP.KD.ZG.

20. OnAsset Intelligence, http://www.onasset.com/index.html.

21. Jean-Paul Rodrigue and Brian Slack, "Intermodal Transportation and Contain-erization," Hofstra University, accessed July 20, 2017, https://people.hofstra.edu/ geotrans/eng/ch3en/conc3en/ch3c6en.html.

22. 99% Invisible, "The Climate-Controlled Shipping Containers That Transport Our Food Are Called Reefers," Slate.com, September 9, 2015, http://www.slate.com/ blogs/the_eye/2015/09/09/reefers_the_temperature_controlled_shipping_containers _that_transport_our.html; World Shipping Council, accessed March 30, 2017, http:// www.worldshipping.org; List of ports that ship food: "Key Ports and Carriers in the Global Food Supply Chain, *Food Logistics,* September 26, 2014, http://www.foodlogistics .com/article/12002254/key-ports-carriers-in-the-global-food-supply-chain.

23. "Overcapacity Expected to Plague Container Lines for Years," Joc.com, September 20, 2016, http://www.joc.com/maritime-news/overcapacity-plague-container-lines -years-analysts-say_20160920.html.

24. "About the Industry: Container Ship Design," World Shipping Council, accessed July 20, 2017, http://www.worldshipping.org/about-the-industry/liner-ships/container -ship-design.

25. David J. Eyres and George J. Bruce, *Ship Construction* (Oxford: Elsevier, 2012), https://books.google.com/books?id=Np7cyt0AFnIC&pg=PA312&lpg=PA312&dq =what%27s+a+ship+cell+guide?&source=bl&ots=Ewedz2ysm9&sig=dc-JwCZAYiyLFc GFUsqxTYB-rcw&hl=en&sa=X&ved=0ahUKEwir2qfSt87RAhVQ9WMKHSBvAIQQ6 AEIHTAA#v=onepage&q=what's%20a%20ship%20cell%20guide%3F&f=false.

26. "Technical Specification for a Typical Steel Dry Cargo Container, 20'x8'x8'6" Type 'Side Door,'" Steinecker Containerhandel, 2012, http://www.steinecker-container.de/container/Container2/Spez-Container/Spez_openSide.pdf.

27. "Bagged Coffee in Containers: Risk of Condensation," International Trade Centre, accessed July 20, 2017, http://www.intracen.org/coffee-guide/logistics-and-insurance/bagged-coffee-in-containers-risk-of-condensation.

28. "Container Climate," Transport Information Service, accessed July 20, 2017, http://www.tis-gdv.de/tis_e/containe/klima/klima.htm.

29. John W. Markham III, Dale J. Bremer, Cheryl R. Boyer, and Kenneth R. Schroeder, "Effect of Container Color on Substrate Temperatures and Growth of Red Maple and Redbud," *HortScience* 46, no. 5, 721–726, http://hortsci.ashspublications.org/content/46/5/721.full; Pakarada Premtitikul, "Is the Colour of a Shipping Container Important?," Inter Dry Moisture Control, October 9, 2010, https://interdry.wordpress.com/2010/10/09/is-the-colour-of-a-shipping-container-important.

30. Dan McCue, "Reefer and Trailer Manufacturers Raise the Bar, *Food Logistics*, August 16, 2016, http://www.foodlogistics.com/article/12240183/reefer-and-trailer-manufacturers-raise-the-bar-transportation-sector-report-august-2016.

31. "Naturaline," Carrier United Technologies, accessed July 20, 2017, http://www.carrier.com/container-refrigeration/en/worldwide/products/Container-Units/NaturaLINE.

32. Bill Mongelluzzo, "Shippers Await Short-Haul Rail Option to LA-LB Ports," *Journal of Commerce*, April 27, 2016, http://www.joc.com/rail-intermodal/shippers-await-short-haul-rail-option-la-lb-ports_20160427.html.

33. "Port of Entry: Houston—Port of Houston Impact to the Texas Economy, 2015," Comptroller.Texas.gov, accessed July 20, 2017, https://comptroller.texas.gov/economy/docs/ports/overview-houston.pdf.

34. Wolfgang Lehmacher, Mark Gottfredson, and Gerry Mattios, "Why the New Silk Road Needs a Digital Revolution," World Economic Forum, January 13, 2017, https://www.weforum.org/agenda/2017/01/china-new-silk-road-bumpy-ride/.

35. Juliette Jowit, "Blimps Could Replace Aircraft in Freight Transport, Say Scientists," *Guardian*, June 30, 2010, https://www.theguardian.com/environment/2010/jun/30/blimps-aircraft-freight.

36. Bruce Chadwick, "Will the Blimp Make a Comeback?" *Boys' Life*, April 1987, 17, https://books.google.co.uk/books?id=hGYEAAAAMBAJ&pg=PA17&lpg=PA17&dq=history+food+blimps&source=bl&ots=BOf07xzyM&sig=bX47adQqGnox3Y6BmLHj6MtScgA&hl=en&sa=X&ved=0ahUKEwjSyrfrv7XRAhUkLMAKHfHGCFYQ6AEIVTAI#v=onepage&q=history%20food%20blimps&f=false.

37. Joseph D. Blackburn and Gary D. Scudder, "Supply Chain Strategies for Perishable Products: The Case of Fresh Produce," *Production and Operations Management*, March 2009, https://www.researchgate.net/profile/Gary_Scudder/publication/227520884_Supply_Chain_Strategies_for_Perishable_Products_The_Case_of_Fresh_Produce/links/0f31753c6c1b1015b8000000.pdf.

38. Jennifer McKevitt, "Southern Ports Aim to Revolutionize Food Supply Chain," Supply Chain Dive, October 5, 2016, http://www.supplychaindive.com/news/port -food-supply-chain-south/427594.

39. K. C. Conway, "Southern US Ports Step Up to Meet Reefer Demands," *Journal of Commerce*, September 27, 2016, http://www.joc.com/international-logistics/cool-cargoes/ southern-us-ports-step-meet-reefer-demands_20160927.html.

40. Chris Scott, "Fresh Route for Latin American Produce," *Inbound Logistics*, August 21, 2015, http://www.inboundlogistics.com/cms/article/a-fresh-route-for-latin-american -produce.

41. Ibid.

42. Ron Nixon, "Obama Administration Seeks to Overhaul International Food Aid," *New York Times*, April 4, 2013, http://www.nytimes.com/2013/04/05/us/politics/white -house-seeks-to-change-international-food-aid.html.

Chapter 5

1. Laura He, "Insurtech Giant ZhongAn Plan to Use Facial Recognition, Blockchain, to Monitor Chickens," *South China Morning Post*, December 10, 2017, http://www .scmp.com/business/companies/article/2123567/blockchain-and-facial-recognition -zhongan-techs-recipe-changing.

2. "The Walmart Distribution Center Network in the United States," MWPVL International, accessed July 20, 2017, http://www.mwpvl.com/html/walmart.html.

3. Derik Andreoli, Anne Goodchild, and Kate Vitasek, "The Rise of Mega Distribution Centers and the Impact on Logistical Uncertainty," *International Journal of Transportation Research* 2, no. 2 (2010), 75–88, https://depts.washington.edu/pcls/ documents/research/Goodchild_RiseOfMegaDCs.pdf.

4. Rich Demuro, "On-Demand Food Apps Use Algorithms for Faster Delivery," KTLA, April 10, 2017, http://ktla.com/2017/04/10/food-apps-use-algorithms-for -faster-delivery.

5. Beth Kowitt, "Prediction: The Food-Delivery Bubble Will Pop in 2016," *Fortune*, November 25, 2015, http://fortune.com/2015/11/25/food-delivery-online-ordering -app-bubble/.

6. Kate Taylor, "Walmart Wants to Walk into Your Home and Put Groceries in Your Refrigerator," *Business Insider*, September 22, 2017, http://fortune.com/2015/11/25/ food-delivery-online-ordering-app-bubble/.

7. Colonel Chris Burke, in discussion with Robyn Metcalfe and Daniel Peacock, Fall 2016 (interview).

8. "Donated Food for Hurricane Sandy," FEMA.gov, November 20, 2012, accessed July 10, 2017, https://www.fema.gov/media-library/assets/images/67186.

9. Ken Lovett, "Gov. Cuomo Order Makes It Easier for Water to Reach Needy New Yorkers," *NY Daily News*, November 4, 2012, accessed July 10, 2017, http:// www.nydailynews.com/blogs/dailypolitics/gov-cuomo-order-easier-water -reach-needy-new-yorkers-blog-entry-1.1692675.

10. "Sysco Eastern Maryland Disaster Plan 2011," Entegraps.com, January 31, 2011, accessed July 10, 2017, https://www.entegraps.com/files/live/sites/contentmaster/files/Private/Education/Disaster%20Preparedness%20Guide/sample-sysco-disaster-plan.

11. "Hurricane Sandy Advisory #14,"American Logistics Aid Network, accessed July 10, 2017, http://alanaid.org.

12. Europol, "Largest-Ever Seizures of Fake Food and Drink in Interpol-Europol Operation," Europol press release, March 30, 2016, https://www.europol.europa.eu/content/largest-ever-seizures-fake-food-and-drink-interpol-europol-operation.

13. Bill Whitaker, "AgroMafia," CBS News, January 3, 2016, http://www.cbsnews.com/news/60-minutes-agromafia-food-fraud.

14. "Q&A: Horsemeat Scandal," BBC News, April 10, 2013, http://www.bbc.com/news/uk-21335872.

15. "Supply Chains," Food Protection and Defense Institute, accessed July 20, 2017, https://foodprotection.umn.edu/research/supply-chains.

16. Hema Vithlani and ICC Counterfeiting Intelligence Bureau, *Countering Counterfeiting: A Guide to Protecting and Enforcing Intellectual Property Rights* (Barking, UK: ICC Publishing, 1997).

17. Food Protection and Defense Institute, https://foodprotection.umn.edu.

18. Bill Lambrecht, "Honey Smuggler Busted, but Many Others Evade Authorities," *Houston Chronicle*, March 29, 2015, http://www.houstonchronicle.com/news/houston-texas/houston/article/Honey-smuggler-busted-but-many-others-evade-6166982.php.

19. Yanzhong Huang, "The 2008 Milk Scandal Revisited," *Forbes*, July 16, 2014, https://www.forbes.com/sites/yanzhonghuang/2014/07/16/the-2008-milk-scandal-revisited/#63cb31534105.

20. Kimberly Warner, "Oceana Reveals Mislabeling of America's Favorite Fish: Salmon," Oceana, October 2015, accessed January 15, 2017, http://usa.oceana.org/publications/reports/oceana-reveals-mislabeling-americas-favorite-fish-salmon, 2.

21. Demian A. Willette, Sara E. Simmonds, Samantha H. Cheng, Sofia Esteves Tonya L, Kane, Hayley Nuetzel, Nicholas Pilaud, Rita Rachmawati, and Paul H, Barber, "Using DNA Barcoding to Track Seafood Mislabeling in Los Angeles Restaurants," *Conservation Biology*, April 2017, doi: 10.1111/cobi.12888.

22. Clear Labs, https://www.clearlabs.com.

23. Chris Elliott, "Elliott Review into the Integrity and Assurance of Food Supply Networks—Final Report," HM Government, July 2014, https://www.gov.uk/government/uploads/system/uploads/attachment_data/file/350726/elliot-review-final-report-july2014.pdf.

24. *Wired* Staff, "Seafood Express: Getting Mediterranean Fish to Las Vegas—Fast," *Wired*, September 21, 2009, https://www.wired.com/2009/09/st-vegasfish.

25. Mary Catherine O'Connor, "IoT Hits Pay Dirt Where Needs and Capabilities Align," Supply Chain Dive, January 24, 2017, http://www.supplychaindive.com/news/IoT-logistics-manufacturing-business-needs/434606.

26. Ibid.

27. Mary Catherine O'Connor, "How Glanbia Uses Asavie's Tech to Connect Fleets, Factories, Farmers, and Retailers," IoT Journal, accessed July 20, 2017, http://www.iotjournal.com/articles/view?15055/2.

28. "PT300 Package Tracker," Sendum, accessed July 20, 2017, https://sendum.com/pt300-package-tracker.

29. Vanee Chonhenchob et al., "Measurement and Analysis of Truck and Rail Vibration Levels in Thailand," *Packaging Technology and Science*, 23, 91–100, http://digitalcommons.calpoly.edu/cgi/viewcontent.cgi?article=1048&context=it_fac.

30. Desert Farms Camel Milk, http://desertfarms.com.

31. For a detailed description of how recalls work within the supply chain, see John M. Ryan, *Validating Preventative Food Safety and Quality Controls, An Organization Approach to System Design and Implementation* (Cambridge, MA: Academic Press, 2017), 241–208.

32. "Multistate Outbreaks of Shiga Toxin-Producing *Escherichia coli* O26 Infections Linked to Chipotle Mexican Grill Restaurants (Final Update)," Centers for Disease Control and Prevention, February 1, 2016, https://www.cdc.gov/ecoli/2015/o26-11-15.

33. "PulseNet & Foodborne Disease Outbreak Detection," *Centers for Disease Control and Prevention*, accessed May 2, 2017, https://www.cdc.gov/features/dspulsenetfoodborneillness/.

34. "Fast Facts about PulseNet," *Centers for Disease Control and Prevention*, accessed March 1, 2018, https://www.cdc.gov/pulsenet/about/fast-facts.html.

35. US Department of Health and Human Services, "Guidance for Industry: Product Recalls, Including Removals and Corrections," US Food and Drug Administration, November 3, 2003, https://www.fda.gov/Safety/Recalls/IndustryGuidance/ucm129259.htm.

36. Lauren Unnevehr, "Food Safety in Food Security and Food Trade," International Food Policy Research Institute, accessed March 1, 2018, https://ageconsearch.umn.edu/bitstream/16033/1/vf030010.pdf.

37. "RASFF: Food and Feed Safety Alerts," European Commission, accessed July 20, 2017, https://ec.europa.eu/food/safety/rasff_en.

38. "Animal and Plant Health Inspection Service," US Department of Agriculture, accessed July 20, 2017, https://www.aphis.usda.gov/aphis/home.

39. Corie Brown, "The Companies Trying to Track Everything We Eat, From Seed to Stomach," *Fast Company*, September 8, 2016, https://www.fastcompany.com/3063134/food-safety-track-and-trace-data.

40. Mike Cherney, "Bankrupt Meat Processor Settles $20M Insurance Spat," Law360, September 30, 2009, https://www.law360.com/articles/125435/bankrupt-meat-processor-settles-20m-insurance-spat.

41. "Consumers Buy Private Brands but Concerns in Food Quality and Safety Point to Need for Greater Transparency," Trace One, September 23, 2015, http://www

.traceone.com/en/news/consumers-buy-private-brands-but-concerns-in-food-quality
-and-safety-point-to-need-for-greater-transparency.

Chapter 6

1. Cainthus, http://www.cainthus.com/#OurMission.
2. Gensler, https://www.gensler.com/research-insight/in-focus/the-gym-of-the-future
-is-closer-than-you-think.

Index